AZURE

WESLEYAN POETRY

AZURE

Poems and Selections from the "Livre"

STÉPHANE MALLARMÉ

a new translation by Blake Bronson-Bartlett

and Robert Fernandez

WESLEYAN

UNIVERSITY

PRESS

Middletown,

Connecticut

WESLEYAN UNIVERSITY PRESS

Middletown CT 06459

www.wesleyan.edu/wespress

© 2015 Blake Bronson-Bartlett and Robert Fernandez

All rights reserved

Manufactured in the United States of America

Designed by Richard Hendel

Typeset in Garamond Premier Pro by Tseng Information Systems, Inc.

This project is supported in part by an award from the
National Endowment for the Arts

Library of Congress Cataloging-in-Publication Data

Mallarmé, Stéphane, 1842–1898.

[Poems. Selections. English]

Azure: poems and selections from the "Livre" / Stéphane Mallarmé;
a new translation by Blake Bronson-Bartlett and Robert Fernandez.

    pages cm. — (Wesleyan Poetry Series)

ISBN 978-0-8195-7579-1 (cloth: alk. paper) — ISBN 978-0-8195-7580-7 (pbk.: alk. paper) —
ISBN 978-0-8195-7581-4 (ebook)

I. Bronson-Bartlett, Blake, translator. II. Fernandez, Robert, 1980– translator. III. Title.

PQ2344. A2 2015

841'.8 — dc23   2015018017

5 4 3 2 1

CONTENTS

Another Mallarmé

It is perhaps because Mallarmé is so important to modernism and twentieth-century and contemporary Continental Philosophy that English-language versions of the poet's work end up inert and academic. The following questions therefore preoccupied us for some time before our labors began: Why can't the English language live up to the demands of Mallarmé's art? Can we make these poems live, in English, without betraying them? Can we practice the art of translation as the art of writing poetry? Or the art of reading? *Azure* is the record of our exploration of these questions through collaborative translation, intensive reading, and our commitment to the process of writing. Mallarmé poses formidable challenges to his translators, his readers, and to poets. We found ourselves meeting these challenges with a challenge of our own. Our primary aim was to create translations that worked as contemporary poems and that linked translation to the reading and writing of poetry. We hope to revive an interest in Mallarmé the poet that rivals the interest in Mallarmé the thinker of poetry.

"—On a touché au vers"

The line given above in French, from Mallarmé's lecture "Music and Letters," demonstrates the way the poet's language, regardless of generic form, resists translation and demands interpretation. Take Rosemary Lloyd's rendering of the line, as published in Mary Ann Caws's *Mallarmé in Prose:* "Poetry has been under attack." What Lloyd's translation captures is the context in which the utterance was made: late nineteenth-century France, several decades after the death of Baudelaire, when the latter had already been canonized as a proto-symbolist hero for the subtle alterations of metrics in his masterful alexandrines (the "feints of his prosody," as Walter Benjamin put it) and his posthumous *Petits poëmes en prose.* But the overturning of poetic tradition in France after 1800 is only one aspect of the "attack" to which Mallarmé refers. The other is the banality of poetic art after 1800, a situation parodied in Baudelaire's mud-spattered poets and dying swans. The decay of the alexandrine and the emergence of modern lyric poetry were born twins, and, true to Mallarmé's utterance, Lloyd captures the pair and leaves the rest to the readers of her translation.

The strength of a rendering of the line carried over by a Mallarmé scholar shines through here. And yet the line must leave out more than just a little of the original French to radiate with the historical significance it eloquently conveys. "*On a* [We have/One has] *touché au* [touched upon/struck a blow against] *vers* [verse]." The tacit allusion to Baudelaire's "Le Soleil," where the poet "go[es] out alone to practice [his] fantastical fencing," is not completely lost, though it is missed. Why? The line represents, importantly, a certain tension conveyed semantically while missing a certain tension at work in the grammar and poetic diction, a restlessness of the signifier. The embattled position of the poet is an embattled position for the singular-plural pronoun (*on*): a whole society that lives in language, iterates it by way of idiomatic expression, and forgets its poetic origins as it falls into habitual, common usage.

To touch upon verse, then, is to rediscover the system of measures and intervals, harmonies and dissonances, with which language begins — the notation systems at work in music as in letters. To strike a blow is to strike a chord: either way, the practitioner's skill emerges from a state of being "en garde," of gaining a heightened awareness of the current context of poetic art and its history — of a sparring with that history and with those who defend their own positions, however conventional or unconventional, in language — and of, at the precise moment, in the precise place, striking. That is what, we have decided, gives Mallarmé a perennial freshness: his strategic positioning and timing.

To elaborate on the specifics of our approach, as well as to highlight our specific contribution to the legacy of Mallarmé, we offer below a comparison of two well-known and respected translations of his verse: Henry Weinfield's (University of California Press, 1994) and E. H. and A. M. Blackmore's (Oxford, 2006). For our comparison, we have selected the first four lines of the second stanza of one of Mallarmé's more difficult and ambitious poems, "Funeral Toast." Above the four lines, the last line of the previous stanza is given in brackets for reasons that will soon be evident. The lines in French read:

[Retourne vers les feux du pur soleil mortel !]

Magnifique, total et solitaire, tel
Tremble de s'exhaler le faux orgueil des hommes.
Cette foule hagarde ! elle annonce : Nous sommes
La triste opacité de nos spectres futurs.

In the first of our four lines under consideration, the word "tel" is used as an indefinite pronoun, rhyming with "soleil mortel" ("mortal sun") and, if not referring to the "sun," then referring to some other masculine noun (nouns being gendered in French and "tel" being masculine and singular) in the poem. This usage is exceptional in French, because "tel" and its variants are more commonly used as an indefinite adjective. A relatively literal translation of the lines would therefore read as follows:

[Return to the fires of the pure mortal sun!]

Magnificent, total and solitary, such/such a one ["mortal sun," etc.]
Trembles to exhale the false pride of men.
This haggard crowd! it announces: We are
The sad opacity of our future specters.

Henry Weinfield translates the four lines as follows:

[Return toward the fires of the pure mortal sun!]

Magnificent, complete within itself alone,
It stands as an admonition to the foolish pride of men.
This haggard crowd announces: We are nothing, then,
Save for the sad opaqueness of the future ghosts we bear.

Weinfield has made several interesting decisions. He captures the sense of Mallarmé's pair of adjectives by transforming "total and solitary" into "complete within itself alone." But the phrase is strictly Weinfield's, not Mallarmé's, for at least two reasons. Mallarmé provides a triad of modifiers: "Magnificent, total and solitary." What the triad amounts to, in sum, is as abstract and as speculative as Weinfield's "complete within itself alone." Nevertheless, the difference between the translation and the original is significant. Weinfield gives his readers a sum, while Mallarmé gives his readers parts. Weinfield achieves this effect by maintaining the first adjective and then presenting the sum of the second and third adjectives with his formulation "complete within itself alone." But that phrase is not in the poem; rather, it is a free translation based on Weinfield's reading of the line.

Such liberties are not taken in vain, however, because Weinfield takes them in order to preserve the original rhyme scheme, which he feels as a translator is the most important property of Mallarmé's verse.[1] We can assume, then, that the new phrase "complete within itself alone" was introduced to preserve the rhyme scheme of the original lines. As mentioned above, the line that precedes the four under discussion ends with "soleil mortel." The complete line in French is "Retourne vers les feux du pur soleil mortel !" Weinfield translates this line as follows: "Return toward the fires of the pure mortal sun!" Because Mallarmé achieves a perfect rhyme between the two lines ("mortel" and "tel"), while Weinfield chooses a slant rhyme ("sun" and "alone"), rhyme may or may not truly be Weinfield's motivation for introducing his phrase "complete within itself alone." So if Weinfield has taken his liberty for its own sake, we applaud him, as we imagine that he would only have done so to carry over into English what literal translation could not.

The second reason we suggest the phrase is Weinfield's and not Mallarmé's is demonstrated in the second line from our sample four. At the end of the first line, the pronoun "tel," which serves as the subject of the verb "tremble" ("trembles," in English), has been moved to the beginning of the second line, so that subject and predicate can be read continuously on one line. This rendering of the line makes way for the new phrase ("complete within itself alone") in the first line, thus allowing Weinfield to remain faithful to his beliefs about Mallarmé's rhyme scheme. And yet the phrase and the slant rhyme are not entirely faithful to the poem. In the second line of our select four, the animated image of the "mortal sun" "Trembl[ing] to exhale" has been replaced by a static monument that "stands as an admonition to," rather than releasing with breath (an essential reference, it would seem, in a poem), "false pride."

Here Weinfield susses out the poem's (denotative, connotative) meaning, brings that across to English, then articulates it in a form that is as close to Mallarmé's as he can get. In doing so, he takes liberties as a translator by forging grammatical continuities where they are complicated by poetic form and by positing speculative images where only traces are given. Weinfield also subtracts peculiar details from Mallarmé's verse, as when he deletes Mallarmé's odd but characteristic use of punctuation in the third line of our sample four. It is as if the translator had no other goal in this case but to render uninterrupted a clause broken in the original by an exclamation point.

E. H. and A. M. Blackmore's translation shares some of the tendencies we find in Weinfield's.

---

1. "What I can say, with absolute certainty, is that in translating the *Poésies* it has been essential to work in rhyme and meter, regardless of the semantic accommodations and technical problems this entailed" (*Collected Poems*, xi).

[returns toward the fires of the pure mortal sun!]

Sublime, total and solitary, then
he fears to breathe out the false pride of men.
"We are," declare these haggard teeming hosts,
"the sad opaque forms of our future ghosts."

The Blackmores offer a variation on Weinfield's fidelity to Mallarmé's rhyme while taking different types of liberties. The Blackmores do not preserve the exact rhyme scheme of the original stanza because the second and third lines rhyme in the original (as in Weinfield's), not the first and second (as in the Blackmores'). However, the Blackmores offer a perfect rhyme ("then" / "men," unlike Weinfield's "sun" / "alone"), and they preserve the cliffhanger at the line break by substituting "tel" with the adverb "then." Taking an original turn with their diction, they keep "total and solitary" intact and suggest "sublime" in place of "magnificent," as if to forego the all-too-easy and direct translation of "magnifique." This choice constitutes another type of liberty: the introduction of a new word, with its own philosophical and aesthetic referents.

Like Weinfield, the Blackmores also introduce a subject before the verb "tremble" at the beginning of the second line. Because "tel" (substituted by "then") is no longer the pronoun for "tremble," the Blackmores offer the somewhat misleading "he" as the grammatical subject of the line. We say misleading because in the translation "tel" is made to refer to the deceased poet, Théophile Gautier, the one being "toasted." The Blackmores' rendering of the line is fair enough. We do not point it out to claim that it is wrong. It is worth noting, however, that the gendered noun in English proposes one interpretation of a line that is polyvalent in the original. By way of contrast, we should prefer Weinfield's "it" for maintaining a wider threshold for interpretation than the Blackmores'.

And yet the Blackmores preserve some of what we hold dear in the original, and what Weinfield withdraws from it, such as the image of the sun "breath-[ing] out the false pride of men," as well as some of the odd use of punctuation. The punctuation in the Blackmores' translation, however, is not Mallarmé's. In place of Mallarmé's "!" and ":" the translators have rewritten the line with quotation marks. Here, the reader may find the extraordinary rendered prosaic. We might even say that these changes not only fail to carry over what is exceptional in Mallarmé's verse but serve to neutralize its most characteristic effects. The quotation marks offer the reader the familiarity of speech rather than breath marked up for pitch and rhythm ("!" and ":").

By various means, Weinfield and the Blackmores succeed most in their translations of Mallarmé's verse when they subdue and constrain its most unwieldy characteristics. No doubt, Mallarmé's poetry still poses significant challenges to the reader in both translations, but these challenges are not always posed by Mallarmé's poetry. As the reader will see in our translations, we have attempted to carry over from Mallarmé's verse some of what Weinfield and the Blackmores did not while taking some of the same liberties. We have dedicated ourselves to the task of doing so — it has fueled our endeavor — as all that we found left out of previous translations increasingly appeared to us to be all that is most important about Mallarmé's work and perhaps even art in general. We cannot undo the formative influence our predecessors have had on our readings of Mallarmé and our translations of his works, but we can excavate the basis for their interpretations of his verse as we carry out the search for another Mallarmé. A case in point: our rendition of the sample four lines in question above may be found to be familiar as well as shocking to readers fond of previous translations of the poet's verse:

[return, return, dear friend, to unfolding light!]

Magnificent, plenary, this
Nothing sucks decorum from the breasts of men.
You pathetic fucks! Confirmed: We are
Frigid echoes, stony elegiac gaze of future specters.

Our rendering of the sample four lines incorporates some of the choices made by Weinfield and the Blackmores. In the bracketed line, we have addressed the "dear friend," Théophile Gautier, who is toasted by the poem. We have, therefore, allowed for a narrow interpretation of the original French, similar to the Blackmores' use of "he" at the beginning of line two. Unlike the Blackmores, however, we follow this narrowly interpreted invocation of the poem's late addressee with a relatively direct translation of "tel" as "this," allowing for the internal rhyme with "magnificent" and the enjambment of "this / Nothing sucks." The line break itself, leaping into the void pressing against it, is consistent with the enjambment of "tel / Tremble de s'exhaler" in the original French; our choice of "Nothing sucks" for the beginning of the second line imitates the visceral character of Mallarmé's image of the sun (if not the poet/poem-as-sun) trembling to be exhaled, or spoken to new life.

Our choice of "plenary" instead of a more direct translation "total and solitary" is in alignment with Weinfield's "complete within itself alone." However, our translation achieved two goals. First, we decided that a noun with a singular-plural semantic value would convey the multiplicity of singularity in Mallarmé's "total and solitary." We also have reproduced, to the best of our ability, the rhythm of the line according to the punctuation — that is, the commas after "magnifique" and "solitaire," which place the "tel" at the precipice of the line break. We were, therefore, able to account for the way syllables in English are stressed or unstressed and are not so in French. That is why "Magnifique, total et solitaire, tel" can have twelve beats (including the ends of "magnifique" and "solitaire") and can also be read at a clip in French. The six beats in Weinfield's "Magnificent, complete within itself alone" carries over the twelve syllables but operates under the laws of English prosody, thus leaving the line feeling more labored than the original.

The music that can be carried over into English, we believe, lies in the briskness of the verse lines, the subtlety of internal rhyme, and the grammatical/rhythmic caesurae of enjambment. So we introduced a sum, "plenary," to convey a brisker movement than either Weinfield's free translation or the Blackmores' direct translation could provide, and we preferred enjambment over end rhyme while maintaining internal rhyme. In these ways, our version privileges a certain music — a *striking* music — that is integral to Mallarmé's poetics and that has not surfaced in previous translations.

Our decision to translate "Cette foule hagarde ! elle annonce :" as "You pathetic fucks! Confirmed:" will, no doubt, trouble some readers. The expletive is not in the original, and the fact that it rhymes with "sucks" in the line above is no justification for introducing it. But that is exactly why we decided to use it: the expletive lends an explicit materiality to the lines, giving semantic value the punctual emphasis of the exclamation point. We have also considered the fact that twenty-first-century readers are likely desensitized to a phrase like "pathetic fucks," which may in fact convey most effectively the frisson of "foule hagarde !" More direct translations, such as "haggard crowd" (Weinfield) or "haggard teeming hosts" (the Blackmores), feel antiquated in ways the line would not have in France in the latter third of the nineteenth century.

We do not want to give readers the impression that our "new" Mallarmé is an edgy, twenty-first-century Mallarmé who curses, spits, fucks, shits, drinks, and goes dancing on Friday nights, though he may very well have done all that and more. Rather, we have insisted throughout our translations that sensation coursed through Mallarmé's verse in its own time.

The reader will notice at this point that the gambles we have taken arise from our conviction that Mallarmé has not yet received his proper due in English and that enthusiasm for his work pales in comparison to readers' appreciation for the French luminaries preceding him, such as Baudelaire and Rimbaud. These two icons of the nineteenth-century fringe owe much of their continuing presence to their notorious excesses, especially their experimentation with hallucinogens. Baudelaire's *Les Paradis artificiels* and Rimbaud's "dérèglement de tous les sens" set the bar for trailblazing misbehavior in philosophy and the arts from the early to the late twentieth century. Mallarmé, on the other hand, has always been associated with the most perverse of the art-for-art's-sake movement and the most hermetic symbolism in Second Empire France. And yet, if what is most important about Baudelaire's and Rimbaud's drug use is the metaphor it posits — as poetic art, too, can change one's mind — then Mallarmé knowingly follows the precedent set by his forebears and perhaps even ups the ante by experimenting further with the transformative powers of poetic art and the magic of the verb. True, his verse is less intent on tying poetic language to intoxicants, but we feel that, although references to intoxicants are less explicit, the important role they play in his verse, as it follows in the tradition of his predecessors, has been lost in previous translations. We have, therefore, erred on the side of updating and emphasizing references to intoxicants and intoxication in our translations. To cite one example, where Mallarmé in "Alms" speaks of how "Tobacco's orisons wordlessly rise and flow, // And powerful opium shatters the pharmacy!" (trans. Weinfield), we hear "And cigarettes make prayers, // And the Oxys make the shelves shatter." We have sought to give the contemporary tongue its due with "cigarettes," "prayers," and "Oxys" (Oxycontins), and by folding the "wordless rise and flow" of the cigarette smoke back into the truncated "cigarettes make prayers." Our decisions were necessitated by the fact that we also see and hear Damien Hirst's *Pharmacy*,[2] big pharma, its integrated networks of production and distribution, and the destroyed lives of addicts, just as pressing and present today in America as they all were in nineteenth-century France.

What we have added to previous translations, we believe, is only what has previously been forgotten in the movement from one national language to another. We have sought to carry over the shock of (historical and aesthetic) rupture that the mastery of form, subjectively conceived, cannot suppress, because it is inscribed within its conditions — because poetry itself is conditioned. Our intention is not to displace our predecessors — we openly admit our dependence on the precedent they set. What has been most important in our trans-

---

2. Hirst notes that "in a 100 years' time this will look like an old apothecary." Damien Hirst, *I Want to Spend the Rest of My Life Everywhere, with Everyone, One to One, Always, Forever, Now*, reduced ed. (London: Booth-Clibborn Editions, 2005), 24.

lations has been our commitment to Mallarmé's sensibility and originality, his freshness and strangeness, and to the poems' ability to stand on their own and to strike, as poems, as the originals do, in English. We sought to maintain an ethos of fearlessness, respecting Mallarmé's own wild gambles. Our goal is to make poetry that exceeds both poet and translator to become the very name of intervention.

On the Logic of the Present Edition

For this edition, we referred to the 1998 Éditions Gallimard *Œuvres complètes* and allowed it to dictate our selection of the poems in verse. As the editor of the Gallimard Mallarmé, Bertrand Marchal, puts it, "an edition *ne varietur* of the *Poésies* does not exist, the poet having died before the publication of the Deman edition (1899), which he had begun planning in the early 1890s, and for which he had sent his publisher a maquette in November 1894" (1144). For the Deman edition (1899), Mallarmé's daughter Geneviève added "Tomb (Anniversary—January 1897)," "Homage [Puvis de Chavannes]," and "To you colonist . . . ," all of which Mallarmé had deliberately left out of his planned book of verse. The so-called "complete" Nouvelle Revue Française edition of 1913 added several more poems, created a new section ("Feuillets d'album"), and "corrected" the text. We have therefore followed Marchal's logic in choosing to include only the poems in the Deman edition rather than create a more "complete" translation of Mallarmé's verse, because the Deman edition is "most consistent with Mallarmé's intentions."

Of course, Marchal's *Œuvres complètes* has the advantage of extensive appendices that include not only the poems Mallarmé omitted in his 1894 maquette that were added by various editors later but also the sometimes extensive variations of these poems. For our edition, we decided that the Deman edition offered a practical limit and an aura of purity to our selection of Mallarmé's works in verse. We were further motivated by the fact that previous translations have not (to our knowledge) followed the order and selection of poems found in the 1899 edition. Weinfield proposes a complete edition, as the Blackmores do, so they had no reason to follow the 1899 edition. The Blackmores do offer an ostensibly "pure" section of poems ordered in accordance with Mallarmé's 1894 maquette, but they then place the rest in appendices. Peter Manson's recent edition, *The Poems in Verse*, includes poems left out of the 1899 edition, so that they can be read "in sequence" (278). Treating the Deman edition as a determining textual condition of our own translation has taught us that, for a book whose publication history is so various and impure, it is all the more important to respect the virtues and drawbacks of every extant edition.

That said, our translation of the 1899 edition is accompanied by two further pieces: a new translation of Mallarmé's groundbreaking late poem *Un coup de dés* (*A Cast of Dice*) and the first English translation of a selection from the preparatory manuscript notes toward his visionary, unfinished "Livre" (book). These offerings are meant to serve as neither appendices nor the initial stirrings of a "complete" Mallarmé arrested midflight. We would rather consider them crucial elements of a poetic program, exceeding the binding of our modest edition and yet suggesting, by way of interrelation between the elements, a framework for running with that program. Set beside the 1899 poems, these secondary works reveal intriguing, and we believe important, constellations: a link between the seafaring revelers of the opening verse poem "Salut" and the sinking captain of the *Coup*; the plans for a sort of spectacular book-theatre-church-economy-society in the "Livre" and the theatricality of the verse (especially "Hérodiade" and "Afternoon of a Faun") as well as the *Coup*. The addition of the secondary works also allows us to present a selection of texts that range from experimentation with the constraints of typical poetic form to experimentation with the constraint of the page itself (e.g., the *Coup*), and that also demonstrate Mallarmé's departure from both to create a type of civic cultural space.

We leave it to the reader to weigh the value of our juxtaposition for considering Mallarmé's vision for the work of poets to come. We believe the unorthodox selection and arrangement of the works more than justifies itself through the reward of discovery awaiting the alert reader. But in the end perhaps we would argue that any selection of Mallarmé's work is valid because it all issued from the same visionary poet whose painstakingly cultivated poetics was, and is, of one piece and ultimately fixated on the achievement of one goal, a goal pursued in verse and free verse, manuscript and print: "le monde est fait pour aboutir à un beau livre."

A Note on the "Livre"

The manuscript notes toward the "Livre" that we have included here consist of descriptions of "séances": theatrical spectacles consisting of readings, ballets, and allegorical plays. Though the word has been translated elsewhere as "session," we have decided to translate "séance" as "seating" because, where theaters begin seating their audiences at a certain hour, performances are not, to our knowledge, typically referred to as sessions. Also, "seating" underscores the thought Mallarmé gave to the seating plans for the theater in which the "Livre" would be enacted, as schematic illustrations found throughout the manuscript demonstrate. We played with the idea of using "setting," thinking the word might refer to seating, musical settings, and the set of papers bound together into a volume all at once. But this idea was symptomatic of the concept at work in Mallarmé's manuscript, not our work as translators. For whether the "Livre" itself is a material text, a theatrical space, or a manufacturing process is left ambiguous throughout the poet's notes.

Ultimately, the manuscript appears to work out a program through which the unattainable Ideal of poetry can be collectively enacted in material reality. The manuscript notes provide diagrams not only of the seating plans for the theater of the "Livre" but also of its thematic elements, the practical measures to be taken for producing editions, or "volumes," of the "Livre," as well as the price of a ticket to one of the seatings. The reader may have some difficulty keeping relations between material and imaginary elements parsed — that is, between those in attendance and the pages of a volume, the reading of texts and the spectacles taking place in the performance space, the performance space and material editions of the "Livre." This difficulty extends to Mallarmé's use of words in the manuscript, as it does in his published verse and prose.

The words "feuille" and "feuillet," referring to a sheet of loose-leaf paper, have been standardized in our translation as "leaf." Only occasionally have we felt it necessary to differentiate between "sheet of paper" and "leaf." We found "leaf" to be the most fitting supplement, for it is clear that the "leaf," referring specifically to that single bibliographic element consisting of two sides, a recto and a verso, is fundamental to the logic of Mallarmé's manuscript notes: the symmetry of diagrams and seating plans, of the schedule of performances, of the oppositions acted out by characters in the spectacles onstage. In what at times reads like speculative ruminations, Mallarmé's conceptual apparatus can be reduced to the simple, material fact that every single piece of paper has two sides.

And so do letters and words. There is a play of the signifier in the manuscript notes that is not cultivated for aesthetic effect but that seems to be taken for granted in the poet's world. In the original French, there is an ostensible conflation of the abbreviation "f" for "feuille" and "f" for "franc," the now outdated French currency denomination. We have not been able to accommodate this conflation in our own translation and have opted to preserve "franc" where the reference to the economics of the "Livre" is clear. Abbreviations of "feuille" and "Feuillet" as "f" in the original French have therefore been rendered as "lf" and "lvs" at some cost. The same can be said for the abbreviation of "volume" as "vol," which can also mean "theft" and "flight." We imagine that the abbreviation of "volume" as "vol" refers to the material editions of the "Livre" in the narrow sense, and we have preserved that sense alone. It is worth considering, however, that this abbreviation takes two possible semantic directions in French. "Theft," in particular, is crucial to the "Drama" staged during the seatings, of which more in a moment. Where the sense of "vol" as "theft" seems to be clearly in play, we have attempted to preserve it.

The fact that one leaf equals two pages and that a leaf can be folded to make two leaves and then folded again, and again, leads to another difficulty in understanding the content of the manuscript notes: its mathematical equations. These equations formalize process and product by calculating the number of pages in each edition of the "Livre," the number of books produced for a print run, the number of persons involved in each seating, and occasionally the economics of the endeavor. The biggest obstacle the equations impose on interpretation is their inconsistency; Mallarmé was still working out the logistical problems involved in the execution of his Grand Œuvre ("Great Work").

Because the "Livre" in manuscript is just over 250 pages long, we have had to select excerpts for *Azure*. We largely based our selections on Bertrand Marchal's notes on the "Livre." He identifies four sections providing the core themes, events, and activities orbiting the project envisioned by the poet:

1. Leaves 24–27, which describe an allegorical stage play, the central character of which receives a "word" or is "called." The character's response to this call is double: he acts as if he is going to obey but never does, "like a recalcitrant child." He may be deceiving the one who calls him, and thus defying the call; he may be deferring a response, and thus being indecisive. Whatever the case may be—however ambiguous—the character is immobilized by his self-contradicting response to the call. This character, the Hero of Mallarmé's Drama, is a new Hamlet who must break free of ambiguity and act.

2. Leaves 28–38, which describe a spectacle in two acts, with an entr'acte. In the first act, two groups of dancers reach toward each other from opposite sides of the performance space, representing conflict, loss of innocence, and time. This allegorical ballet of division and desire establishes the symbolic foundation for the spectacle to follow. Without actually dividing the first and second act, the entr'acte creates a sense of transition by way of a curtain, light effect, and music. The second act consists of two scenes, described on leaves 34–35 and 37–38. Leaf 36 marks the transition between the two scenes, yet another transition without certain disruption. The first scene takes place in the "magnificent and sad vision" of a dead city, a sort of ruin decimated by time or plague. The "desert" or "void" has taken the city over, leaving it in the past and anticipating the poet of the future: the decisive Hero. The setting appears to occupy the "between" temporality facilitated by the theatrical event of the

"Livre" itself. The second scene is foreshadowed, literally, by a play of shadow and light on a curtain or scrim. What ensues is a kind of circus, beginning with savage animals that are transformed into an orderly parade of beasts with women on their backs.

3. Leaves 41–47 present two opposed figures, an old priest, embodying religion deprived of the hope of transcendence, and a young man, who seems to have been immaculately conceived and aspires to pursue the work to come — the birth of a new world. This young man appears to be the new Hero of the "Livre," now referred to as the "Operator" of the "machine" or "device" driving the Drama.

4. Leaf 220 returns to the Operator and his Operation, or what appears to be the work of bringing the "Livre" into existence. Echoing the "call" of leaves 24–27, leaf 220 presents the Operator with an "invitation," serving as a modernized type of poetic inspiration issued by a Muse. The Operator's union with the Muse takes place through the ritual of "nuptials" and the consummation of the marriage to follow. The nature of this operation is described in leaves 122–123, where the operation is the action that must be carried out in order to attain something that, once attained, will be abolished. In this case, that something is virginity — prized, sought, and lost in that seeking — which is scheduled to be consumed at the nuptial "fête," or "feast" in our translation. The conundrum of whether to consume the female body of inspiration (to take the Muse's virginity and to annul the Idea she inspires in the Operator) or to find some way to carry out the operation without committing violence against the object of poetic desire (at this point, it seems, the choice to defer action) echoes the dilemma of the Hero of leaves 24–27. Leaf 220 proposes an allegorical operation that will not resolve the conundrum so much as it will give it yet another ritual of enactment: the Muse veils herself in satin, as the Operator covers her with his silk hat, which next bursts into a new sun. Something like a magician's grand exit through an explosion and puff of smoke, the Muse is saved from the violent fulfillment of poetic desire by a veiling and unveiling, carried out by the Muse and the poet simultaneously (they are, perhaps, two sides of the same leaf). The result is a generalized illumination and the return of a new religious humanity.

These sections constitute the backbone of the selections provided in this volume, but we have included additional material to flesh out these sections and to give the reader a manageable introduction to Mallarmé's vast, unwieldy collection of notes and fragments. The reader will occasionally find pages of the "Livre" in a non-sequential order, as in the last pages of our selection from leaf 250 forward. In these cases order has been given to the leaves for the sake of legibility, and we have followed the French edition in doing so. As the pages of the manuscript are unbound, and as the fragile folded pages may have broken and been reordered through the years, it is possible that the non-sequential order actually restores the original order of the pages as Mallarmé worked on them.

The "Livre" manuscript appears to conceive of a world-making book in all of the impossibility of its true realization, evoking the necessity of its state as a work-in-process, to be explored and experimentally treated. The notes carefully approach the point of conjunction between Idea and Act without subjecting that conjunction to reductive understanding, without presenting the assumption that it has been obtained, possessed, completed, or violated. Our transcription is only a beginning in the process of thinking through the richness of the manuscript notes, especially as they regard a rethinking of the supposed obscurity of the verse poems and the *Coup*. And any textual edition of the "Livre," as Mallarmé knew, could only be a flight from its intended material context of performance and participation, or a theft of that context.

We have followed the lead of our editors at the University Press of New England in restoring graphic elements of the manuscript left out of the French editions of the "Livre." We decided the graphic elements should be restored not for the sake of accuracy and the accurate reproduction of the documents themselves but as part of the interpretive demands the manuscript makes on the transcriber and translator. Connecting lines and bracketed sections add coherence to the manuscript at times and are simply confusing at others. Where these elements hinder legibility, the representation of them is also faithful not only to the composition but construction integral to Mallarmé's "Livre," if not his writing process in general. Whether these elements help or hinder, the manuscript notes themselves can be consulted thanks to the Harvard University's Houghton Library, which has made available through its online catalog digital facsimiles of the entire manuscript. The curious reader will discover features of bibliographic interest in the color images, such as the numerous pages Mallarmé left blank in the manuscript; the way the poet sometimes wrote across the centerfold (one of the provocative devices used also in *A Cast of Dice*); and the material state of hand-folded leaves, formed into booklets (much like those described in the manuscript notes), from which the manuscript is composed. Our selection of excerpts from the "Livre" includes the four sections identified by Marchal as well as a good deal more preceding and following them. We have thereby positioned the sections identified by Marchal in a broader context of manuscript notes that conveys the evolution of the Idea recorded there as well as its inconsistencies and many tantalizing enigmas.

Please note: Sections left out of our translation are indicated with bracketed ellipses. Each translated page of manuscript begins with a code (e.g., {f55 [40(A)]}) in the upper-left corner, which does not appear in the original manuscript but has been carried over from the Gallimard edition.

WORKS CONSULTED

Austin, Lloyd James. *Essais sur Mallarmé*. Ed. Malcolm Bowie. Manchester, UK: Manchester University Press, 1995.

Badiou, Alain. "A Poetic Dialectic: Labîd ben Rabi'a and Mallarmé" and "Philosophy of the Faun." In *Handbook of Inaesthetics*, 46–56, 122–41. Trans. Alberto Toscano. Redwood City, CA: Stanford University Press, 2005.

Benjamin, Walter. *The Writer of Modern Life: Essays on Charles Baudelaire*. Ed. Michael W. Jennings. Trans. Howard Eiland et al. Cambridge, MA: Harvard University Press, 2006.

Blanchot, Maurice. *The Space of Literature*. Trans. Ann Smock. Lincoln: University of Nebraska Press, 1982.

———. "The Silence of Mallarmé," "Mallarmé's Silence," and "Mallarmé and the Novel." In *Faux Pas*, 99–106, 107–111, 165–171. Trans. Charlotte Mandell. Redwood City, CA: Stanford University Press, 2001.

Bowie, Malcolm. *Mallarmé and the Art of Being Difficult*. Cambridge, MA: Cambridge University Press, 1978.

Cohn, Robert Greer. *Toward the Poems of Mallarmé*. Berkeley: University of California Press, 1965.

Derrida, Jacques. *Dissemination*. Trans. Barbara Johnson. Chicago: University of Chicago Press, 1981.

Fowlie, Wallace. *Mallarmé*. London: Dennis Dobson, 1953.

Johnson, Barbara. "Erasing Panama: Mallarmé and the Text of History," "Les Fleurs du Mal Larmé: Some Reflections of Intertextuality," and "Mallarmé as Mother." In *A World of Difference*, 57–67, 116–33, 137–43. Baltimore, MD: Johns Hopkins University Press, 1987.

Pearson, Roger. *Stéphane Mallarmé*. London: Reaktion Books, 2010.

Rancière, Jacques. *Mallarmé: The Politics of the Siren*. Trans. Steve Corcoran. New York: Continuum, 2011.

Robb, Graham. *Unlocking Mallarmé*. New Haven, CT: Yale University Press, 1996.

Ruppli, Mireille, and Sylvie Thorel-Cailleteau. *Mallarmé: La Grammaire et le grimoire*. Geneva: Librairie Droz, 2005.

Sugano, Marian Zwerling. *The Poetics of the Occasion: Mallarmé and the Poetry of Circumstance*. Redwood City, CA: Stanford University Press, 1992.

Sartre, Jean-Paul. *Mallarmé, or the Poet of Nothingness*. Trans. Ernest Sturm. University Park: Pennsylvania State University Press, 1988.

Lloyd, Rosemary. *Mallarmé: The Poet and His Circle*. Ithaca, NY: Cornell University Press, 1990.

Laupin, Patrick. *L'Esprit du Livre: le crime de poésie et la folie utile dans l'œuvre de Mallarmé*. Vareilles: La Rumeur Libre Éditions, 2012.

Mallarmé, Stéphane. *Œuvres completes*. Vol. 1. Ed. Bertrand Marchal. Paris: Gallimard, 1998.

———. *Mallarmé in Prose*. Ed. Mary Ann Caws. New York: New Directions, 2001.

———. *Collected Poems*. Trans. Henry Weinfield. Berkeley: University of California Press, 1994.

———. *Collected Poems and Other Verse*. Trans. E. H. and A. M. Blackmore. Oxford: Oxford University Press, 2006.

———. *Divagations*. Trans. Barbara Johnson. Cambridge, MA: Harvard University Press, 2007.

———. *The Poems in Verse*. Trans. Peter Manson. Oxford, Ohio: Miami University Press, 2012.

———. *[Le livre]*. Manuscript [undated]. MS Fr 270. Houghton Library, Harvard University.

Meillassoux, Quentin. *The Number and the Siren: A Decipherment of Mallarmé's Coup de Dés*. Falmouth, UK: Urbanomic, 2012.

Scherer, Jacques. *Le "Livre" de Mallarmé: Premières recherches sur des documents inédits*. Paris: Gallimard, 1957.

Williams, Thomas A. *Mallarmé and the Language of Mysticism*. Athens: University of Georgia Press, 1970.

Poésies

Then nothing, bright spray, hymnal holiday,
To show us but this skin;
Dead ahead, impacted sirens
Roll perversely: a log of bodies

We set our course, O rangy
Friends, I already at aft,
You at the glinting fore which breaks
The sea's membrane of flashes and shivers

A honeyed drunkenness sends me
Fearless into foundering
Forward with poise to toast

Solitude, reef, star
These which gathered, drew resonant
And plumped the naked canvas of our craft

HEX

Above the harried mortal rabble
Leapt through clearings savage manes
Of sapphire beggars along our path

Banners a black wind unfurled on the march
Scored the flesh with such icy cruelty
That it lifted stranger ruts there

Hoping always to end at sea,
They traveled without bread, sticks or urns,
Biting gold citrons of the bitter ideal

Most expired in midnight processions,
High on images of glutting blood,
O Death the only kiss for sewn lips!

A mighty angel rips their stitching
Erect on the horizon in a sword's flowering folds:
Crimson stiffens in the desiring breast

They nurse at sadness as they nurse dream
And when their fat tears course steadily
The people kneel and their mother rises

They are consoled, assured and majestic;
But drag behind them their 100 scored brothers,
Trash sacrifice of chance and ruin

Salt tears wreck their tender cheeks,
They eat ash with identical self-same love,
However vulgar or idiotic is the taunt of fate

They could also rouse like drums
The *ressentiment* of clotted races,
Peers of an unpicked Prometheus!

No, vile and bone-dry fixtures of deserts,
They are harried by the lash of a furious tyrant,
Hex, death-spell and silent laughter shackling them

He likes it from both ends and all holes, the liberal!
Torrent purged, he slops you in mire
And leaves coupling white swimmers in muddy tangles

Thanks to him, if someone ejaculates through his horn,
Children trap us in obstinate laughter
As, fist to ass, they simulate fist-fuck Huzzas

Thanks to him, if someone adorns a sunken chest
By pinning a rose to it which, nubile, revives it,
Drool will glisten on the condemned bouquet

And this midget skeleton, styled with feathered cap
And boots, whose armpit hairs stream like maggots,
Is for them an infinity of disaffection and pain

Angered they would provoke the perverse,
Their shiny new blade following moonlight rays
Which pack snow in its carcass and criss-cross it

Desolate and without the pride that sanctifies misfortune,
And depressed by defending their bones from pecking birds,
Animus takes the place of regret

They are the joke of scrapers of base instruments,
Of urchins, of harlots and of the ancient order
Of dancing street kids when the bottle is drained to the last

The poets good for pity or vengeance,
Not understanding what's wrong with these absent gods,
Call them stunted and unsound

"They flee, having had enough,
As a virgin mare the tempest foam,
Sooner than part in clanking, gallops

We will gorge the victor with incense at the feast:
But they, why not take them up, these actors,
Whose scarlet exhalations scream stop!"

When all the rest have spit on them disdainfully,
Null and in wisps of base words of prayer for thunder,
These heroes in excess of touching misfortune

Will hang themselves ludicrously from street lamps

APPARITION

The moon, sullen. Teary seraphim
Dreaming, bow in hand, in calm of misty
Flowers, drew from dying violas
White sobs evacuating across blue corollas.
— Your kiss present at the birth of a world.
My loving zero, martyrizing me,
Tears the bell-ringer, despair, perfume
That without regret or dregs
Crusts the pipe with potent resin.
I wandered thus, my eyes on the stones
When, sun rushing through you, in the street
And at evening, you appeared to me laughing
And I thought I saw the maiden with the sun-grail
Who, in the drowsy roilings of a spoiled child,
Always used to pass, releasing from unclosed hands
A flurry of white bouquets, bloom of perfumed stars

HOPELESS PLEA

Princess! jealous of the fate of a Hebe
Who rises up along his cup to steal a kiss,
I extinguish my fires but am only a poor abbot
And will not figure naked on the Sèvres porcelain

As I am not your bearded spaniel,
Pastille or rouge, or childish game,
And since on me your gaze has fallen,
Blond whose divine coiffeurs are goldsmiths!

Name us. . you for whom so many peals of
Raspberry laughter combine in your very own troop of lambs
Grazing on everyone's vows and bleating my delight,

Name us. . so that Love winged with a fan
Paints me with flute in fingers lulling this flock,
Princess, name us the shepherd of your smiles

THIS WORKED-OVER CLOWN

Eyes, lakes reborn with pooling drunkenness
Far from the actor whose gesture evoked
The shivering black plumes of gas-lamps—

I ate a window through a wall of canvas
My treacherous swimmer's leg and arms,
In multiplied lengths, saying to hell with that shitty
Hamlet! It's as if, in the tide, I improvised
A thousand dead grottos in which to, virgin, disappear

Hysterical gold cymbals in crazed fists,
Suddenly sun pierces the nudity
Blazing from my pearly freshness,

Night of skin sloughing off and puss gallons,
Not knowing, ingrate! that it was my sole hope,
This greasepaint drowned in glacial waters of evil

WINDOWS

Done with hospice, and with the stink
Rising along bland white curtains
To the outsized crucifix stranded on the wall,
This moribund hustler straightens his flaccid back

Less to keep his carcass warm
Than to see a little sun on the cobblestones, to press
Against the glass the strands of his frail
Frame that a shaft of light would lend some color

His mouth, watering for the Azure —
As when, once young, it sucked up bounty,
Sapphire hymnics, once upon a time! — streaks
With a long, bitter kiss the window's hive

Drunk, inflamed, he forgets medicinal oils,
Sheets, the clock, the acrid bed,
The cough; and when night washes over the rooftops,
He sees in dancing twilight

Golden prison ships — swans
Drowsing in a fragrant, purple river —
Rocking their bright, savage tackle
In magisterial aloofness, flush with memory

Thus, seized with revulsion for any pig
Wallowing in fat comfort (his every appetite
Sated), who roots around in filth
To offer filth to the sow suckling his little pigs

Thus I flee and cling to the window's cells
Where one can turn one's back to the world, and, shagged
With evening's dust, bathed by ageless waters,
Anointed with Infinity's daybreaks,

Reflected I see myself an angel! and I die, and I love
— Whether the window is art or the mystic —
I am reborn, wearing my dream-diadem,
In originary skies where Beauty flowers!

Yet, alas! Flesh is master, captivation
Crushes, nauseates me in this playpen,
And a regurgitated spray of Idiocy
Forces me to close my face against this sky

O You, who know bitterness, is there a way
To break this Antichrist-defiled crystal
And to flee, with my two naked wings
— At the risk of endless, eternal plummet?

FLOWERS

Of golden avalanches from sapphires, o day
And of the permafrost of stars
Once you unlatched prodigious calyxes
For the earth, still young and unbreached,

Tender gladioli, trim-necked swans,
And this divine laurel of exiled souls
Vermilion naked toes of seraphim
Blushing with dawn's prudishness,

Hyacinth, myrtle in charming daybreak
And, similar to her flesh, cruel rose,
Hérodiade blooms in manicured gardens,
Streaked by wild and radiant blood!

And you've made the lilies' plaintive white,
An ocean of sighing, drift across
Bands of smoking sapphire: horizon
(They climb airily toward a weepy moon)

Hosannah strings and fragrant ashes,
Our lady, hosannah garden of limbs!
Echo's ouroboros comes complete through celestial nights
Dissolving ecstasy's shrouds across us

O Mother, from your center, just
And powerful, glass calyxes hold
Black incense of Death and hold futures
For that poet whose marrow's scraped clear

RENEWAL

Sickly spring's sadly chased
Winter, season of hard art, serene and lucid,
And in my center where mournful blood has its throne
Ennui stretches

Remeron-white twilights
A circle of iron encloses an old tomb,
And, mournful, I wander after a dream like lavender
Through fields of immense strutting juices

Then I fall, annoyed by arboreal perfumes, weary,
And for the dream digging a ditch with my face,
Biting warm earth where the lilacs grow,

I wait, sag-collapse, dragged under by boredom . . .
— But laughter's Azure glints on the bush and in the flight
Of so many birds that blister and chitter in the sun

ANGUISH

I'm not here tonight to break that castle, o beast
Sin thickened, don't want to dig
No grave in your filthy hair for my gushes
Of terminal ennui, my kiss smoking:

I want death's sleep in your bed
And to lurk under repression's veils
In the aftertaste of your black frauds, you
Who know more of nothing than the dead:

For depravity corrodes gold bones,
And has, like you, clipped me,
But while your stone torso's occupied

By a heart unscratched by crime's tooth,
I flee, blood drained, defeated,
My waxen brother haunting me,
And I fear the ancestors as I sleep alone

*

Tired of my indolence,
Crown for which I'd once fled a childhood
Of rose forests under purple skies,
And seven-knotted weary of the hard pact
Of digging, at daybreak, a fresh grave
In my brain's greedy, cold town,
Gravedigger, no pity for wormlessness,
— What to say to the Dawn, Dreams, visited
By roses when, in fear of such livid roses,
This vast cemetery stitches together empty holes? —
Let's unmoor from viciousness
And, smiling at rebukes of friends, the past,
Genius, and my lamp that sees me writhe,
Imitating a heart of Chinese silk and water
Whose ecstasy paints the end
On lunar cups of snow, so perfect,
Of a flower, weird, scent saturating his life,
Naked, flower sensed, child,
Its soul-blue filigree eats a way through.
The wise can't see, serene,
So I'll choose a young province
That I'll also paint on cups, half-interested.
An azure strip, thin and whitish,
Would be a lake on porcelain horizon,
A ribbon lost in a stark cloud,
And soak its sedate horn in water's crystal,
Not far from three pinkish, big, emerald eyelashes

THE BELL RINGER

Clear bell chimes
In the pure clear and deep morning
Passing over a child murmuring an angelus
In lavender and thyme

The bell ringer, brushed by some pigeon,
Hanging sad and whispering Latins
On the stone that tightens the worldly rope,
Hears only a far-away twinkle scratch him

I am he, oh. These nights of wanting,
So hard to pull the rope and chime Ideals
As faithful wings extend their cold sins

And the voice comes in chips and heaves!
But, one day, having hit the note, o Evil,
I will free this block, hang myself

SUMMERTIME SADNESS

Sun on sand. Sunstroked, sleepy hustler.
Your gold hair's undulant warm blonde,
And burning incense from your every cheek,
Love's concoction's mixed with tears

Of this white phosphorus ribbon the immutable
Has made you say, sad, o my wet kisses:
"We will never be one mummy, singled,
Beneath ancient desert and rustling palms!"

Her hair's a warm, flooded Nile
In which to calmly drown soul's obsession
And find that Nothing you don't know

I will taste your streaked eyelids
To see if it gives to the heart, that beats for you,
The indifference of azure and stones

THE AZURE

Of Azure, fixed. Serene irony overwhelms,
Lovely laziness like flowers,
The poet, abject, who curses his gift
Across dead desert pain

Fleeing, eyes closed, I feel it watch
With the fever of earthen guilt,
My soul, nothing. Where to go? And what sad night
To throw, in tatters, across this overpowering contempt?

Up! Up! Smoggy clouds pour your monotone cinders,
Gusts of billowing yellow smoke, into the sky.
Let's drown this livid morass of autumns
And build a vast mirror: silence!

And you, mindless in filth, clean up
To see these pale roses in the mud,
O Ennui, to play with a worker's hand
The huge blue holes, glint-evil, birds make

Again! Let the chimneys smoke
Forever, on, and a nomad prison, ash,
Snuff with its dragon's tail
The sun slicing itself up on horizon

— Sky's dead. — Toward you I run. Give, o
Heaviness of all things, forgetfulness of the Ideal
And of sin, to this martyr who sojourns
Among the sweat of mortal cattle

I want out. My empty brain, empty
As a pot of face paint at the wall's foot,
Dry, empty, it can't face paint, mask, a weepy idea
Shuttling some girth toward pinned eyes. .

Vain! Azure triumphs. I hear it sing—
In the bells, my soul—sings, scandal
Of Victory and should-not-be. Terrifies;
Surges up from living metal in seraph-sapphire

Rolls in on the fog. Ancient. Crosses
That inner rift like a steady cleaver.
Where flee this revolt, useless, perverse?
I am haunted. Azure! Azure! Azure! Azure!

SEA BREEZE

Sad flesh. And I've read all the books.
Adieu. Go down below. I feel like birds are drunk
On hanging around the unicorn's froth and sky.
Nothing, not old gardens in the eyebanks,
Will box up, tidy, a heart sloshed at sea.
O nights! Nor the lamp's Sahara
On empty paper,
And not the sixteen-year-old nursing.
Fuck this. Steamship tipping your mast,
Lift anchor for nature's exotics!
I'll slough off Ennui by being cruel
And I'll believe again in the supreme farewell of handkerchiefs!
Maybe the masts, which want storms,
Storms where the wind bends its knee over shipwrecks
Lost, mastless, mastless, nor fertile isles . . .
Dear heart! Hear the song of these watchers of the sea

SIGH

Soul to forehead where night cinema, o calm sister,
An autumn surging stingray-red edges,
And to your eye of tents and deserts, angels,
Climbs, in a chilly purple garden,
Faithfully, a sighing leaping waterjet, straight to Azure!
— To mellowed Azure of October,
Which mirrors in huge pools its infinite whatever
And drags, on still water whose windy
Gray heaped leaves drag agony into a furrow,
A long ray of sun behind it

ALMS

Eat it, you beggar,
This succorless dried-up titty of demented nourishment.
Suck glass, shard on shard

Lift evil, like black caramel, from this platinum
And, vast as us, in fistfuls, let's kiss it, huff
Till it twists — and with fuck-all relish

Censors burning, all the walls
Harbor a blue so clear,
And cigarettes make prayers,

And the Oxys make the shelves shatter.
They look good, luxed, bare thigh, and you want
To strip off that satin and drink it off in joyful waves

Do you wait for morning by princely cafes?
Frescos of nymphs and vials
Press their feasts toward beggars

And when you go, old god, shivering under skeins,
Dawn's a pool of gold wine,
And you've a star stuck in your throat

You miscalculated. Your ecstasy's early.
At least you can light yourself a little plume
At mass to the saint to whom you're always crawling back

I ain't taking shit.
Earth opens its old self to the starving, yes.
I despise other alms. Just forget me

Whatever you do, brother, don't go buy bread

THEIR DESIRABLE GIFT

Here's a child of Idumean night!
Naked, featherless, black, pale wing blooded
Across glass washed in oils and golds
And through icy panes, oh. Again ruined,
Sunrise threw herself on an angel-shaped lamp.
Palms. And when this strange artifact
Sees the eye of some sneering father,
Solitude, blue and antiseptic, tremors.
Coddler, with your She and innocent cold feet,
Welcome something awe-inspiring, terrible.
Your voice's part viola, part harpsichord.
With some runty finger do you poke your instrument
From which should flow, in sibylline whiteness,
She for whom the pure Azure starves?

HÉRODIADE
Scene

THE NURSE — HÉRODIADE

N.

Alive! Or is that royal among the dead?
Bring to my lips your fingers, their rings, and stop
Your march on unknown horizons. .

H.
                                    Back.
This hair's perfect blonde ice
Freezes me singly in dead fear,
And my locks, light-spun, are immortal.
Woman, your kiss would tear through me
If death weren't beauty. .
                        By what infatuation
Driven and what oracle-uprooted morning
That pours its sad bacchanals on sundowns,
Do I know it? You've seen me, o succor of winter,
Tred down into the zero of iron and stone
Where my aging lions dragged savage epochs
And I walked, fatal, hands folded,
In a musk of Pharaohs:
Don't you see my fear?
I stop, dreaming of exile, and I cut,
As by a pool where jets of water bend for me,
The pale lilies in me; entranced,
I follow their nonchalant leavings
Step by step through dreaming, in silence,
As the lions share my heavy robe
And watch my toes play succor to the sea.
Stop. Your sad, smeared flesh;
Come. My hair like a too-savage
Style plumping manes for panic,

Help me, since you can no longer bear
To nonchalantly comb my hair in the mirror.

                    N.

If not leaping amphorae of myrrh
Then distillates of withered rose,
And shall we, my child, give
The funeral rite a chance?

                    H.
                Leave them! Know
That I hate them, and would you have me drown
My bliss in their intoxicants?
I want my hair, not of flowers
That erase misery
But of gold forever
Untouched by perfumes,
Embossed with devilish smiles, and wan,
To see then the sterility of star blood,
Bands reflecting you, blades, and vases
Of my solitary childhood.

                    N.

Forgive me, ageless one, your prohibition forgotten
By my spirit grown pale as an old book or dark. .

                    H.
Stop! Put the mirror there.
                    Mirror!
Chilled pool, ennui shard fixed
Where often, for hours,
Dreamless, searching memory,
Like leaves spread under glass, abyss gapes.
There I came to myself, a strange double.
Night is evil's, and in your stark fountain
I have seen my naked other broken up!

Nurse, am I fine?

N.

A star.
Whose lappets fall and tangle.

H.

Stop! Crime
That makes my marrow icy, repress it,
This gesture, grave sin: tell me
What devil births the worm of this mood,
This kiss, these proffered musks and, dare I say, o.
O my heart, this hand that founded evil,
For you wanted Children of the Sun to stand in day
Which will not end without devastation's banners. .
O tower, Hérodiade crumbles, seeing it!

N.

Strange days. And heaven help you.
You wander, sojourner, fury pent
Seeing in yourself an evil augury;
Still, as charming as you are immortal,
O my child, and only frissons and such
That. .

H.

Would you not touch me?

N.

I would love
To know the one who conceals your Fate.

H.

Enough!

N.

Will he come someday?

H.

Pure stars,
Don't listen!

N.

How, except among some rare
Umbrage, to dream even more fearlessly
And as a servant of the god for whom
Your grace waits! And for whom, anguish-
Withered, do you guard the spiraling black lash
Of your being?

H.

For myself.

N.

Sad flower blooming careless, alone
Or bent to her watery reflection, watched to exhaustion.

H.

Go, keep your pity — your irony too.

N.

Tell me: oh! no, naïve child,
This haughtiness will wilt. .

H.

But who would touch me? Lions?
As for the rest, I want nothing human and, sculpted,
If you see me with eyes pinned,
It's in reeling remembrance of your breast milk.

N.

Fate's sad plaything!

H.

Yes, it's for me, myself alone, that I flower!
You know it, amethyst gardens, receding
Endlessly in abysses of thought,
Ignored ores, guarding your light
Under the sleep of ancient earth,
You, gems from which my eyes
Borrow their dancing clarity, and you,

Hammered golds that give my locks
Death's sheen and inescapable allure!
As for you, woman born in evil times
To the hazards of sibylline grottos,
Who speaks the word: mortal! for whom, from my
Robes' bunched calyxes, dragged scent of raw delights,
Would show a bit of my white, my naked flesh,
Portending that if the sun's weak blues,
For which woman, stupidly, would darken her flesh,
Sees me in my wrapped veils, a star,
I die!
   I love the uncut hymen and I want
To live in the deathluster of my shine
For, at night, reclined on my bed, coiled
Inviolate, sensing in senseless flesh
The gasp of your light's marrow,
You who self-slaughter and burn, chaste,
Night of white floes and unforgiving water!

And you, solitary sister, o my eternal sister,
My dream will climb to you: already such,
Unbelievable limpidity of a heart which gathered it,
And think myself alone in this stale fatherland,
And everything lives in idolatry thus
Of a mirror reflecting in her sleeping calm
Hérodiade, diamond etched. .
O condemnation. Yes! I feel it: I'm alone.

N.

Has death come near?

H.

No—

Be calm, take your distance, and forgive this hardened heart,
But first, if you will, shut the shutters: seraphic
Azure smiles in the windowpanes,
O lovely Azure! I detest you.
       The waves
Are calm, and do you know a country, far away,

Where the ominous sky has Venus's teeth-grit,
She who, at night, burns in the leaves:
I want to go there.
                          Shine again, childhood,
Speak flames where wax under warmth
Sheds among dumb gold some unfamiliar tear
And. .

                          N.

        Now?

                          H.

        Goodbye.
                          You lie, o naked flower
Of my lips!
                I await the unknown
Or, maybe, ignoring the mystery and your cries,
You drop supreme and deadly tears
Of a childhood feeling among dreams
That sorts out, at last, its cold stones.

THE AFTERNOON OF A FAUN
Eclogue

THE FAUN
May nymphs bubble over.

So clear,
Like blood fountains, their color misting
The drouse, bundles of slumber.

Did I love a dream?
My doubt, night's tremble of prehistory, is confirmed
In many an intricacy of twig, which, the real wood itself
Demurring, proves, christ! that I alone proposed
For my victory a crown of roses —

Let's reflect. .

As if these women needed
Are desire's phantoms! Faun,
Phantom troops emerge from blue,
Dead-eyed, grief drowned, from the brightest:
And the other? All sighs. Is she then
The opposite of warm sun on wool?
Not that! But, awe-struck, drained, immobile,
Fever breaking on her head, sauna, and struggle
No water murmurs, not streaming, save from my flute
In the bush blushing with accords; and the only wind's
Out the two pipes ready to spill before
And drip sound in fever droplets,
Its, the horizon not flexed a crease,
The calm breath visible, *poiesis,*
Of spirit's flame aligned with heaven.

O Sicilian shores, gentle swampland
Of my satanic devastations, envy of suns,
Unspoken under corollas of light, SAY IT

"How I cut here the thorn, rose mastered
By genius; when, on the scabbed gold of distant
Greens, giving vine to fountains,
Billows a tent of wet white silk:
And how in the beginning of song
This swan's clatter off, no! of naiads skimming
Or plunging. ."
                  Inert, all burns in the savage hour
Without traces, by means of which art detailed
Too much to be cut — hymen — for the one reaching *la:*
So would I wake to the first urge,
Upright, alone, under a tinted light-ribbon,
Lilies! for ingenuity, one among you all.

Other than zero modulated by lips,
Kiss which, traitor, insures hell,
My heart, untouched, yet bears
The strange proof of some god's tooth.
Wait! to such constellations raised among
My inexhaustible, twinned reed, we played beneath azure:
We who, turning away from worlds,
See, across one long prayer, that we amused
Rock and tree and grass and animal
With strange confusions of heaven and song;
And to love's apex plays,
Away from lust and returns,
Closed eye tracing pure thigh,
A ribboned vanity, droning line.

Do, then, ecstatic instrument, o unholy
Syrinx, flower again in lakes where you call me!
Me, from my pride masks, I'll speak awhile
Of Déesses; and in pagan images
Undo their belts to get at shadow:
So when, from grapes, I've sucked clarity,
Banished regrets scattered by my snappings,
Laughing, I'll raise in armfuls to the summer sky
Light, ballooning skins, like kites,
Gaze through it all as evening, star strands, shine.

O nymphs, let's inflate, once more, some assorted SOUVENIRS.
"My eye, peering through reeds, speared each god's
Neck, which then cools the sting in waters,
And anger makes the canopies tremble.
And the splendid lily disappeared
In clarities and gasps, o stones!
I run; when, at my feet, entangled (dying
In their serpent's stiffened languor),
In each other's quilled arms, the sleepers;
I take them, without unlocking them, and fly
To this wall, hated by mottle's stupidity,
Of wild rose sunstroked, willing last musks;
Such the same at day's end our struggle."
I adore. O savageness of virgins,
Red balloon, burden, savored, nude,
Gliding from my lip which sips fire
And in torn sheets! flushes flesh's dread:
From inhuman tread to the skittish heart
Which opens onto innocence, wet
With exposure's mad, despairing heaves, at least.
"My crime lies in having, pleased to quell split-tongued
Fears, shredded the messed bouquet,
Of kisses the gods kept so tidy.
For I anguished to hide this thrum smile
Under the whispers of she alone (holding on,
With bare finger, so that her candor
Kept itself in ripples of a sister's shine,
The child, naïve and unblushing):
As from my arms, undone by uncertain trespass,
This prey, ingrate, is delivered pitiless
On my sobs, still breathless."

And there it is! On to new fortunes, trailing
Tresses knotted to my horns:
My passion, purple and already ripe —
Every pomegranate bursts and murmurs with bees;
And our blood, electric to whoever eats it,
Flows for the panoply of eternal swans, desire.
At the hour of tinted gold and ash

A feast perfects itself beneath magma flecks:
Aetna! it's you, visited by Venus,
Ingénue whose talons stick with lava,
When thunders are quieted or flame dies,
This queen's mine!

        O certain hubris. .

              No, but the soul
Of empty speech and leaden body
Submit, late, to noon's bright silence:
Spent, I must sleep on burning sand,
As I love, open-mouthed, star's decantings!

Sisters, adieu; I go to see your shadows stretch.

*

Lock of hair, lifted, flame-carved
To lengthy Occidents spreading their Cs,
Heads with tongues (for sure wilting crowns)
And of the crown, say flame's primordial gnashing

But, without gold, sighing this colored swell
Kindling Promethean fire ever
The first the last standing
In the glint of vertical-pupiled disdain

Raw nakedness of heroes. Defames.
She, neither constellation nor flames at her fingers,
Just woman gloriously so
And in a twisting of her head's minaret

Rubies sewn, doubts singed
And a joyous, tutelary torch

SAINT

So window's eye's hidden
And frayed sandalwood adorns
Nauseated viola
Tingling with flute or mandolin

Is the saint, spreading
The ancient book, unfolding
A Magnificat of diving silks
Long ago at vespers and compline:

At this window-eye's sagging glass
That brushes a harp by the Angel
Formed with its flight of evening
For a delicate phalange

Of the finger, that, without the old sandlewood
Nor book, the harp balances
In its fletchings, musician, harvest
Of silence, o black apples of silence

FUNERAL TOAST

Gautier, death-glyph, sign of our shared happiness!

Abyssal tribute — hollow offering!
Do not believe that in this mausoleum's occult hereafters
I raise my empty glass in which a golden serpent tightens!
For me your apparition will not suffice:
I've set you myself in a Malebolge of crystals.
The rite exists for our hands to snuff the torch
Against the tomb's colossal iron doors.
And we, invited to a quite simple feast
(To sing the absence of the poet), cannot ignore
This well-wrought prison that circles him entirely.
If this is but the bright victory of a moment,
Respite against the hour of stinking, vile perfidy,
As naked evening floods us with its color,
Then return, return, to unfolding light!

Magnificent, plenary, this
Nothing sucks decorum from the breasts of men.
You pathetic fucks! Confirmed: We are
Frigid echoes, stony elegiac gaze of future specters.
But I've despised the gnashing of banners that eat through plaster,
The lucid terror of a name,
And when, deaf to my hymning and unafraid,
One of these oblivious passersby — proud, blind,
And silent — with skin like moldy wafers — becomes
A Christ and cenotaph of our eventual interment.
Abyss borne through a fog of crystals
By the hornet's cloud of the poet's silence,
Nothingness to this ruined man of yesterday:
"Vistas unrecoverable, o thou, what is the Earth?"
— Trembles this dream; and, voice shattered,
Space has, for its toy, a cry: "I do not know!"

The Master, eyes keen, has, as he goes,
Slaked an Eden of restive wonder,
And his singular death rattle resurrects
For Rose and Lily the mystery of poetic founding.
Is there nothing left of this call?
Friends! Forgive my black cynicism.
Genius is a disc of unobstructed light.
We are the thirsty flowers of its star.
And I know the labor undertaken
To transmit this nourishment, and our privilege
To drink in its unhurried apocalypse
Of speech, purple ivory and great clear calyx,
That, rain and diamond, the diaphanous look
Dotted there on these flowers, none of which fade,
Isolates among the hour and the break of day!

Already in the day's true groves
Where the pure poet signals
So as to interrupt the dream that destroys
His repose, death sets the task:
Bury your eyes. Your fountains will
Become rushing tributaries through this tomb,
Cold dragon that conceals death
And greedy silence and huge darkness

PROSE
for des Esseintes

Hyperbole! Can you not lift
From my memory an occult
Canticle for our age, triumphant
If illegible, as from a sealed grimoire?

For through alchemy I inscribe
Hymns on the souls of men
By the work of my patience:
Atlas, herbarium and rituals

Our eyes walked
(I promise we were two)
Over many rustic charms,
O sister, likening theirs to yours

The age shudders with the Law's withdrawal
When, grasping at nothing, one says
Of this shadowless eye which our
Twofold unconscious unravels

That, gradient of a hundred irises,
They know in fact its site once was,
Stripped now of the name that tastes
Of the issue of summer's golden trumpet

Yes, on an island the air has charged
With vistas, not hallucinations,
Each flower unwrapped itself
Without our even asking

As, immense, and again
Contoured with lucid dilations,
Such a trough was cut
Between it and the gardens

Glory of commitment, Ideas,
Everything in me shone to see
That family of irises
Surging up to this fresh task

But this sister, sage and tender,
Did no more than smile,
And thus to know her better
I cultivate my antique art

Oh! Spirit of struggle, know,
At this hour of our silence,
That heavy crops of lilies
Grew too wild for our knowing

And not as the shore cries
When its droning pleas
Beckon plenitude to fatten
Into my youthful astonishment

Hearing then sky and cart
Endlessly testify on my path,
Across the swallowing current,
To this country's never-having-been

The child shrugs off its ecstasy
And, already hardened by trial,
She speaks the word — CORPUS —
Born for eternal parchments

Before a tomb her ancestor,
In any weather, laughs
At the name concealed
Behind the ponderous gladiola

FAN
of Madame Mallarmé

With, as for language —
With just a flutter's
Unlatched the future word
From its priceless casement

Wings on low the carrier
This fan if it is
The same, behind which through
A mirror dilates

Clear (where will fall
Pursued in each grain
An invisible bit of ash
To my chagrin)

And thus it flashes
Between your peerless hands

OTHER FAN
of Mademoiselle Mallarmé

O one who dreams, so that I who unsheathe
In pathless ecstasies
Know, by a subtle lie,
To keep this my wing in hand

Twilight's panes
Break over you with each flutter
From which winds, held back, commence
Their fine stampede of horizons

How space
Stretches out like a great kiss
Which, mad for satisfacting,
Finds no shore

A vertigo of wild paradises,
Like a pinned scoff,
Snags the corner of your mouth
Then flows over its single band of folds!

Rose coasts roll pink scepters
Where dead, gold nights burst Eastward;
Yet this sealed, unstamped flight's posed
Against a bracelet's specks of fire

SCRAP, AS FOR AN ALBUM

Suddenly, as if kidding,
Mlle. who waited
To hear, unwraps a little
Of my muscled flutes' wood

It's like this effort
Of drawn pastorals
Perked up once I stopped
To take your gaze in mine

Yes this my wasted breath,
Until at the very limit,
Set by my pitiful dexterity
Can't imitate

Such a raw, clear
Childlike laughter
Releasing air-Valentines

REMEMBRANCE OF BELGIAN FRIENDS

The breathless hour carries
Black rot like black incense,
And like the stench made visible I sense
The stone revealing itself fold by fold

Delivering nothing
No evidence of succor
And we, enconstellated ones, so "poof"
About the sudden grip of friendship

O you so near in Gravitrons of
Bruges multiplying dawns at the defunct canal
While swans in numbers pad off

When, solemn, this ancient city informed me
Who among her sons another flash
Of irradiated white's designated like egg-of-the-stealth
To drop from the Spirit's wings

STREET SONG

I

(The Shoemaker)

Besides tar, nothing can do,
Lily born white, or perfume
I prefer it simply
To such rich salve

He adds leather,
More than I had ever,
Mind a tire-iron bent
To sandals and bare soles

His steady hits
Push nails' crudity
Into flesh that wants it
And the *clang clang clang* is other

Sole remaker
Oh if the dancer's tongues
Were only right to your pitch!

STREET SONG

II

(Herb Vendor)

As for that blue-hearted lavender,
Don't think this clipped
Lash is on the market
For just any coward

Who papers walls
Of absolute places
For stomachs that burn
At being reborn blue glass

Better placed live like an insect
In a thick head of hair; here, stick it,
Its heart's-blue draft will sooth
Zephirine, Pamela

Or bring to your heart's other,
Faithful one, this heart's
Percept of buds

TICKET

No preliminary blows,
Nothing like the streets
Subject to the black flight of hats;
But the vision of a dancer

Whirlwind of muslin or
Spare fury in spumes
Her knee, lifting,
Our mutual origins

For all, except her, *ad nauseam*
Spiritual, drunk, immobile
Striking in her tutu
Stirring her bile

No laughter lifts the air
Of her dress, but Whistler

TUNE

So alones (choose)
Swanless, dockless,
Soaked in nothing—
In this glance pocketed

Here, about that
Halo that's out of reach,
Are such turning skies
Of every color

But easy springs
Linens pilfered
Some cormorant that plunges
Thus exaltingly aside

In broken surface tension
You become naked jubilation

TUNE

II

My drives'
Diamond dice, cast
And lit, lost,
Snag fury, silence

Stranger's voice
In the brush,
Bird heard only
Once, only once

The poet,
Whose dubious exhalations
From my breath, not his,
Heaves in a coward's sniveling

His self, shredded, to some
Alley drags off his pitiful banners

VARIOUS SONNETS

When shade, with Law's white cobra split thru it
Old Nightbooth, cock and blood of my vertebra,
Vampire and fire ants under funeral boards,
Doubtless folded its wing in me

At the hotel found myself, where to seduce an emir
Lilies and celebrities are Medusas and long necks—
Your imperious brow, stitched with shadow steaks
In the eyes of one, who with flower, faith, wilts

Indeed I'm sure, in this nontime, this night, that Earth
Vomits Peles and black gods, thunderous,
Seen clearest through centuries' gels

Space, self-identical, stretched, negating,
Traces nausea's rivulets, brilliant floes, seen
And morning's star leaks pus, celebration, genius

Vivacious, pretty hymen
Cuts, a straight-razor wing on mend
All lake of ice bye-bye, Snow White under chilly boughs,
Glacier seen through to outspread wings!

Leda pushes the swan's neck back
And the god glances; still, care not—
Gives no hope, having neither sung sterility
Nor pierced winter's splendid ennui

Its long neck will tremble white pain
Of space stretched inturned the ungiving bird,
Muck of plumage trapped in ice

Phantom, crystal coffin to have,
Fixed in contempt's icy virtuals that,
With this one, uncanny, conceals all Swan

Suicide. Good death or beauty?
Victorious either way. Victory's ember,
Blood froth, cloud of Venus flytraps and gold
O laughter, send down your purple ribbon

As from the hand of a queen to my nothing tomb
Yes? For all this shine, not even purple's delayed
And it's midnight, shadow roasting us. Except . . .
A head's false crowns spills seed of icy, spiritless stone

Yours. And so delight always! Yours alone,
Yes, you who of the disappeared sky retains
A cock's feather for your stupid cap

Clarity: When you lay it in furs,
Soldiers' coffin of bad seeds, indicating you,
And clarity will have shed from skin of roses

Her pure nails so high, consecrating their onyx,
Anguish, this midnight, supports, torchbearer,
Vesperal dreams burned by the Phoenix,
Not gathered in the cinerary amphora

On credenzas, in an empty salon: no ptyx,
Abolished trinket of inane sonorousness,
(For the Master has gone to draw tears from the Styx
With that object for which Nothing is honorous)

But near the crossing in the vacant north, an ore
Tortured perhaps to match the décor
Of unicorns charging the fires of a nix,

She, stripped, dejected mist in the mirror, even
Though in this oblivion, frame-enclosed, is fixed
The coming cinquefoil, sext chiming, for our septet

TOMB OF EDGAR POE

As, at last, shaped into Eternity,
The Poet rises with sword drawn,
His century aghast for having missed
That death triumphed in this strange voice!

The people, shivering hydra, hearing this angel
Give a purer sense to the language of the tribe,
Contemptuously pronounced it a derangement fueled
By the vile currents of some black liquor

Strife between sky and soil, o grief!
If our imagination does not sculpt a bas-relief
To ornament the dazzling tomb of Poe,

Calm block voided from some obscure disaster,
May this granite at least forever mark a boundary
To black flights of Blasphemy dispersed into the future

TOMB OF CHARLES BAUDELAIRE

The buried temple shits from its sepulcher's
Mouth — a sewer drooling mud and rubies —
Some rabid idol Anubis,
Its fiery muzzle a savage bellows

Now that the gaslight turns out louche tongues,
Shameful exposure of our syphilitic transactions,
It haggardly illuminates an ageless pubis
Whose flight comes to rest under the streetlamps

What dry leaves, in cities of votive light,
Could give as well as she the blessing
Of a little ass resting against the marble of Baudelaire?

In a veil that rings the nothing with tremors,
She, his shade: a cloak of poison air
We breathe in even if it kills us

TOMB

(Anniversary—January 1897)

The black anguished rock the wind rolls
Will not stop, not under pious hands
Grasping its resemblance with human evils
As if to bless some funeral mould

Almost always, if the wild pigeon coos
This intangible grief-membrane lowers
Concealing the red star of tomorrows
Whose shining bathes us in silver

Who seeks, pursuing the solitary leap—
Till now beyond our vagabond—
Verlaine? He is hidden in the grass, Verlaine

With no surprise but complicity
In the lip, hot furrow
At the shallow stream, death

HOMAGE

The luster of an already funereal silence
Binds voluminous folds into an armature
Whose principal pylon crumbling
Incites memory's aid

Our stale victory struggles in this magic,
Hieroglyphs exalted by the thousands,
To charge the air with a familiar frisson!
Sooner drain it from me with a gramophone

From the smiling first scuffle,
Disdained by mastering light, has sprung,
Toward a threshold birthed for their simulacrum,

Deafening gold trumpets, reeling on vellum,
The god, Richard Wagner, irradiating a sacred
Evil killed with ink, in sibylline sobs

HOMAGE

Each Aurora, even wrecked
An obscure fist clutching
Clarions of azure
Played deaf

Has the shepherd with his flask
His baton whipping hard
All along his future path
Ample source of ecstasy

Future perfect, how you live
O solitary Puvis
De Chavannes
                    never alone

Peaking at sunset
With the nymph with no veil
Your Glory uncovers

*

To you colonist with a splinter
That billows over splendid-vex, India,
This salute is a messenger
Of time twice around the tip

As on a low crossbar,
In plunge with the vessel,
From which dragonfly wings
Gather a foam of new annunciation

Which droned endlessly
While fixed rudder
In a wrong turn,
Foams black, despair and rocks

Reflected in its droning:
The sneer of our unburnt Vasco

I

All Pride it smokes the night,
Torch in a muffled agitation
Without the immortal puff
Being able to remain in the state of abandon

Heir's ancestral quarter,
Abyss gilded, but a prize falls
And would hardly distend
A hallway by its return

Dread, necessity of cause,
Holding in its talons
Disavowed death

Under thick marble, it isolates
The concave flame
Of that sparking counselor

11

Surging from behind and bounding
From candied glass licked down
Bitter dawn is — no unfolding,
Throat stalled, and what?

Yes, believe two mouths didn't
Drink, neither lover nor mother,
Of that same Chimera, I,
Sylph of horizons

All vase, not for drinking
But for handfuls of husband ash,
Twitches, yet says No,

Diamond studded mourning kiss!
All, falls for nothing, says
The rose is shadow wrapped

III

No lace
Can't believe this incredible joy
And won't ironize it, open,
No more than a tossed mattress

We all agree this struggle's bland
And garland's the same
And fled from white glass,
More floating than buried

Still, in place of the dream-crowned
A mandolin sleeps, sadly,
In the mandolinist's empty pocket

As if some window,
From no tones but his own,
Brotherly, might have been born

What balm-of-time-silk, tissue
Where Chimera's chambers unlock,
Equals the thunderhead's odalisqued *there*
Which, in the mirror, you hold hand to palm

Moth-eaten windowshade, hermetic,
Admired by passers-by:
Me, I have your naked braid
To bury untroubled eyes

No. Mouth guarantees
Not the least bit of taste,
If he doesn't, your Romeo,

In heavy tufts,
Exhale, in diamond baguettes,
An abdomen suppressing Glory-heaves

Straight to your story,
Lunatic hero, fool
Touching some mound
With your bare toe

That moraine's from
Glacial eyebands, and I
Know only the Absolute
And laughter uncontrollably

Say then I'm not joyful,
Supercell lice of rubies
Tearing singes in the air

Empires
And like worm-
                split purple, spoked eyes
Of the chariot wheel's single sunrise

Red fire lozenge
Heave of basalt, lava
Slave's lung dimples back
Evil's stretching filigree

What tomb's storm (you
Know it, slathery, and foam)
Supreme among wrecks
Shatters (re-shatters) bare mast

Where the one whose bright wrong
On the slopes of perdition
Splits blister mirror abyss

White stingers trailing
Greedily will have drowned
The siren's infant belly

Leaves seal the name, Paphos;
Makes me laugh to choose with exactness
A ruin, sprayed by countless waters
Under hyacinths, distant, of kingdoms

Cold floes, scythes
I won't inflate with empty rhymes
Should this bone-white clatter, level, reveal no
Phantoms, kingdoms lost, and no dignity of backdrops

I'm slaked on no fruits here
Nor those of fine cannibal tooth:
A flash of aromatic, human flesh!

Foot on some mound, love slips
I sit a bit and think, lost, perhaps — perhaps —
In nowheres, magma breast-heave of a distant Amazon

A Cast of Dice

A Cast of Dice never will abolish Chance

by

STÉPHANE MALLARMÉ

A CAST OF DICE

NEVER

WHEN EVEN THROWN IN SOME CIRCUMSTANCES
:RNAL

FROM THE DEPTHS OF A SHIPWRECK

BE IT
    that

        the Abyss

whitened
    spreads
        furious
            under an incline
            glides desperately

                    on win
                its

nce foundered from evil while taking flight
                    and covering the jets
                            cutting at the root the bonds

        very much internally recollects

e shadow flown in the deep by this alternate sail

                        until adapting
                                to the span

            its gaping profundity like the shell

                    of a ship

            leaning to one or an other side

THE MASTER

surged
    inferring

                in this firest

                        th

                  as one men

        the unique Number which can

                        hesi
                  corpse by the

sooner
    than to play
        like a hoary maniac
           the game
        in the name of the waves

                  shipwreck

        outside of ancient calculations
    where the hand-work forgotten with the age

            once he grasped the helm
is feet
        of the dead horizon
ared
that heaves and melds
        in the fist which would hold it
stiny and the winds

n other

                    Spirit
                        to throw it
                            in the tempest
                folding back the divide and passing proudly

d to the secret that it conceals

des the leader
s like a mane

ct from man

        without vessel
                no matter
                        where vain

ancestrally not opening the hand
clenched
beyond the useless head

legacy in the disappearance

to some one
ambiguous

the ulterior demon immemorial

having
from nowhere places
induced
the old man toward this Last conjunction with probab

this
his puerile shadow
caressed and polished and rendered and washed
softened by the wave and subtra
from the hard bones lost between the planks

born
of a frolic
the sea for the ancestor who tempts and the ancestor against the sea
superfluous luck

Nupti
of which
the veil of illusion stirs up their shame
like the phantom of a gesture

will stagger
will draw down

madness

WILL ABOLISH

AS IF

An insinu

in the si

in some

flu

le

d with irony
                        or
                the mystery
                                precipitated
                                        shouted

l of hilarity and horror

nd the abyss
                        without scattering it
                                        or fleeing

                and cradles the virgin sign

                                                AS IF

feather solitary bereft

roke of midnight that encounters or grazes it
and immobilizes
on velvet crushed by burst of somber laughter

this whiteness rigid

sory

in opposition to the sky
too much
not to mark
narrowly
whoever

bitter prince of the reef

adorns himself with it in heroic fashion
irresistible but continued
by his little virile reason
in lightning

anxious
        expiatory and pubescent

                                        mute

                                The lucid and stately
                                invisible on the bro
                        scintillates
                                then shade
                                a tenebrous little
                                in its siren twis

                        with last impatient s

laughter

    that

       IF

ertigo

t

    time
     to slap
rcated

  a rock

false manner
    immediately
     evaporated in mists

    which imposed
     a limit on the infinite

IT W

stellar

IT WOULD BE

    worse

           no

               more nor less

                                         indifferently but so mu

THE NUMBER

HAD IT EXISTED
as something other than a sparse hallucination of agony

HAD IT BEGUN AND HAD IT CEASED
surging as denied and closed when manifested
finally
by some profusion reduced to barely nothing

HAD CODED ITSELF

evidence of the sum for the fewer than one

HAD IT ILLUMINATED

CHANCE

Falls
    the plume
        rhythmic suspense of the sinister
                burying itself
                in the original foams
    which previously leapt from its delirium up to a summit
                    desiccated
        by the identical neutrality of the void

NOTHING

of the memorable crisis

or was

the ev

ed in view of all results null
                    human

            WILL HAVE TAKEN PLACE
     an ordinary elevation pours absence

                              BUT THE PLACE
whatever inferior lapping so as to disperse the empty act
          abruptly which if not
     by its lie
          had founded
     perdition

     in these latitudes
                    of the wave
                         in which all reality dissolves

at the altitude

MAYBE

as far as a

with the beyond

                    outside interest
              if accounted for, signaled
                                   in general
ding to such obliquity by such declivity
                                        of fires

     toward|verse
           what must be
                 the Septentrion also North

                                   A CONSTELLATION

              cold from forgetfulness and desuetude
                          not so much
                       that it enumerates
                 on some surface vacant and superior
                    the successive collision
                                        sidereally
                 of an account total in formation

ing watch
        doubting
              rolling
                    brilliant and meditating

                       before stopping
           at some anterior point which sanctifies it

                 All Thought emits a Cast of Dice

From the "Livre"

{f 7 [1]}

~~To finish~~
~~conscience~~
~~And troubles~~ ×××××
~~too much~~ ××××
~~street~~

~~crime~~
~~infamous~~

~~double~~
~~location~~
(~~crowd my~~ /
~~place~~   ~~a crime sewer~~

[...]

{f 15 [6 (A)]}

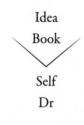

Idea
Book

Self
Dr

Th	Myst
World	Year
Hero	Hymn
Man	Life

{f 16 [6 (A)]}

glory

genius   passion

health
life

{f 24 [12 (A)]}

Always this word of a human language

and that designates someone

    if it ⌐ were uttered

              ⌐ by half
no seems to say that ⌐ which it was

                          him
called,   ~~and in his~~   bending an ear

                            head tilted
           a little raised*   face smiling
on one side,   , ~~and sweeping back~~   as which

    ⌐ listening so as to obey, that which follows
is going ⌐ to obey — ~~and head sweeping back~~   ~~y~~

~~far, com~~

                            <u>Nothing</u>

    all while doing the opposite

---

* for the word seemed to fall into the depths
             come from above
somber
     where he is

to mother

~~showing~~   1
like a recalcitrant child*
~~espi~~ traitor and

head (scission, trestle,) and ~~following~~
~~which follows the body~~ that follows the body from the
side opposite to the possible source of the
sound.

      ~~as which flees also~~
           ~~fearful~~
    ~~that one called it thus enclosed in~~

~~the circle of a word~~   ~~nothing said here of~~
      ~~the soul~~

       ~~mimes~~
     ~~has he some troops~~
     ~~and his mystery~~

---

* he is quite grave however <u>this man</u> — has
the whole stature —

     but vast —

         grave kneels

1

The word is therefore not uttered for him

at this moment when he hears it, if he

ever did (no — he seems to say to

this doubt, recognized ~~the~~ his open mind — he

not not in the order, which neutral calls it and leaves it free — * ~~this word~~

did not) ~~and he is going to return to~~

proclaimed, this word which is he there and retains him, and all while resting.

pleasure
as if to show it

returning

the attitude, which is that of a departure —

leaning forward, one foot forward

⌐ and mirror ~~summit~~ mountain — with attitude —
diagonal ⌐

but

---

* minus his friends, no chain.
he trembles

2

Without lifting the other foot, however — without
departing, complying with the hidden order in the
firm and auspicious neutrality of this word
           exaggerated maybe the secret defiance of his
       departed act, despite everything
               ~~or maybe is it for   entering~~
                   ~~(crawling)~~
                           ~~and shadow, block~~

     ~~of~~
~~in defiance and piety~~

                               defiance
                       that someone — this
                   will not be him

                           once summed
                   by this word and knowing who
                   he is.

                           (strength
                               of a word well said

                   or maybe

                       is it for

{f 28 [16 (A)]}

It's always you that I

see on the shore

this time with glory and bitterness in the past ⌈ so as to recommence
~~despair~~ ⌊ the great song

↓
.   when I left...   [or broken
       (they half disappear but not without having yelled
          ↑ women tone of reproach   (mine
        ↑ a lovely country...
          divine earth
        more of a fiancée

.   with deception and glory still
↑   to conquer

        ↑ my only fiancée! the earth
          or fiancée
         and this recurrent dream

---

and interruption to fool the public about both!

the representatives of humanity
today

but without the public know-
the crowd
ing the mystery here presents

in the room inherited know

it the mystery

while hoping

A great fact, audacious flight

of their prejudice

has been accomplished

{f 29 [17 (A)]}

and as there was in the beginning,

in what he was going to repeat,

arms linked, on the shore — and
_____

that he thinks them liberated — they are illuminated

liberated here

~~and from two sides~~
and as from two sides returned to each other, by
                              here and there
an expert ~~interlacing~~ mélange of those

that one has seen from one side then the other, the

double troupe, is there this

_____

appearing there then as half
                    two halves of a troupe

{f 30 [18 (A)]}

time the arms of one side in effect linking arms

with the other, as on two

very ~~distinct~~ shores, distant, ~~and~~
        between which,
but ~~from where~~ across spirit without

doubt [across it], ~~those~~

~~who once wer are there link~~
                and ideal
it operates according to a mysterious relat-

ion, ~~the one which its~~ each one

    linking from where it is, either it

went there or

the arms in its absence

---

                                    hemisphere
                            — and eye of the monster
                            who watches them —

                            ~~but something~~
                            ~~lacking them~~

---

and reverie arms crossed over breasts
                        absent

from the other side, future and past

at the same time ⌠ one arm low, another
　　　　　　　 ⌡ lifted, pose of
　　　　　　　　　 ballerina

　　　~~Such is that which~~

　　　　　Such is that which takes place visible

~~in s~~ omitted

　　　　　　　~~But as it's for they alone that it was~~　　　　　　⌠ For this
and he hears their laughs — you will tell me —　　　　　　　 dream
this, that — diamond — diamond — he only heard　　　　　 was made
that (her, glory, ladies abed, fortune, etc.)　　　　　　　 of their
they ceasing their laughter in the diamond bird　　　　　　 purity
truly appeared — there and that they would like to have everything ⌡ guarded
　　　　　　　　　　　　　　　　　　　　　　　　　　　　　　 for
　　　　　　　　　　　　　　　　　　　　　　　　　　　　　　 all

{f 32 [20 (A)]}

Open on middle of 2nd background (solitary

~~feast~~   in itself — (~~feast~~ that goes

until the before mysterious, as the

background —   — preparation for the feast

=   entr'acte

confusion of the two

—

with interruption of the open background   or = ×
_____   scission in
                                                    the background
                                                    — starting where
=   entr'acte   we left it

before alone
                        (curtain for the feast (regrets, etc.)
and building itself

from the middle

and raising of curtain — fall —   room
                                           and background
        corresponding to <u>background</u>   the beyond

and <u>before</u> mysterious — corresponds to
that which hides the <u>background</u> (backdrop, etc.) makes the mystery.

_____

background = room   * in lusters

{f 33 [21(A)]}

        the electric arabesque

     is lit from behind — and the two

veils

      — emerges from sacred tear of the

veil, orchestra — or tears —

     and two beings at the same time bird

and perfume — resembling both from
    pulpit
above (balcony) com

---

    egg   church

{f 34 [22 (A)]}

sadness of the borderless

Magnificent and sad vision

What is ~~here tr~~ ———— ~~or the~~

The remains of a large palace,

— large as a city — or

of a ~~large~~ city united as a

single palace.

     There is everything the echo says —

double and duplicitous, questioned

by the voyaging spirit (of the wind)

     Everything we say, it's that it

---

unless some new, floating city   triangular
returned — more the city of the future poet   rocking

{f 35 [23 (A)]}

lying in the tenebrous past —

in effect the desert has taken it over —

unless it lies in

the future — ~~impossible~~ closed to the

~~for sudden~~ human eyes, there

~~the void and~~ in the depths

In front — double fountain, where its
                    dream
condemned people — who sleep —, no

longer newly mirrored*

*regarding their immense pride

{f 36 [24 (A)]}

Which could — being the remains in
the past — and what strange adventure
has precipitated thus this race.

Modern is this calm — man dominator
                    ~~function of pre~~
— tell us ~~your~~ the secret

— Meanwhile — dioramic
curtain has gained depth — shadow
stronger and stronger, as hollowed out
by it — by the mystery —
        The scrim has ~~low~~ been surrounded — with —
the gains that music could not bring
and which are there, elephants, etc.

{f 37 [25 (A)]}

The wild beasts have been seen in

effect on the depths of the scrim, in ~~this~~

~~imm~~ this repose [and have not dared
     fire
enter — as if afraid — they have

seen something like themselves,

but invisible, and have jumped —

two times — ~~first a panther~~

~~against~~ as if one against the other

— serpents which hiss at them in

hate, jumped across the serpents'
           movements of
rings, to prove there is no

glass   then suddenly return

---

              the ignorant beasts
but in the middle

{f 38 [26 (A)]}

pacified — and carrying on their backs

~~wom~~ these two ideal

women, ~~pl~~ passed there. (~~they don't dar~~
                         wearing

they dare go no further because

huge fire in the middle, desert

voyager — night tent — from the tent to the

palace — (or boat)

> chasing the two beasts
> the most uncontrollable
> white bear
> black panther
> elephant holding
> both

beasts raised on hind paws, expressing desire
to see! [while one arranges —

{f 41 [27 (A)]}

(1

| and the day will come — when torture bee

ignored — hun prudery — hunger and love
                                    of skies |

———————— the old man —

            under the influence of crowd — that he

            holds it is

                — will appear — to have
    suffered the actual torture —
            guillotine
            fusillade

                    — while dying of
                            hunger
                        or really
                    doubt, all is there
                        has only a cent!
                        hesitates (dinner)
                the two   or
                in Th?,   drinks

hunger of your flesh thirst of your eyes
            finale

(2

to go — "into the trick of death from

starvation" ~~unt~~ if — etc.   crowd ⎡ suffering ignored
⎣ here

until the tomb inclu-

sively

it is — and not

it is fictionally, condi-

tional — (literarily)

he commits himself to it, to show

what will happen if...

but she must
according to him, for
death by starvation gives him the right
cover herself   {   to begin again — another star, summit —
skies...

— after however

victim of his trick

fallen skies
did the wind close the

door (old story — castle)

the priest?

——— emerge from confinement

1/2

and playing there with his amassed

force — for it's in the idea
(unjust
of being condemned to death that he

amasses it — skies —

free thought in itself.

c. to d. having done

as priest deprived of everything

---

priest must ignore, for human glory, the mystery of
woman — where (child in her arms) all will be resolved
by that

{f 44 [30 (A)]}

(4

but the trick (from which: to us, two, etc.)
is that not found mystery sought (if not helped, crowd?)
and that it is only there in tomb that he can find it
from which —

on the other hand youth is essential

in him delivering himself to the dream of starting up the great

machine, a worker

man — ~~comes~~ (but who

is only old — ~~com~~ comes

in tomb   (burying there fiancée
priest — confinement
unknown)   to know

mystery   , before   getting married

— what to say to children

———   source   — old man

fight — and there everything played

worker left behind
old man escaped —

_____

you are already thinking about that? about them? —
It's strange   love, you.
— leave this to care of ancestor?

{f 45 [31 (A)]}

———— that young man comes sacred

in death — the mystery of love —

———— he this other need

⌈ let's unite our two needs

————————————

and the old man emerges

existing — for it's old age —

fictive Death —

as youth is fictive

birth.

he emerges ideally — not in reality
and without friends or parents, not in the thoughts of others
but in his own — he believes — or of crowd*

— the door has closed — for

the spring is on the other side — he has no

right, etc. to these skies —
we have one⟩   mystery —
that if ⟨found,   now are cloistered

there to find, for to know the mystery
                        there must be death

⎡ so the trick ⎤
⎣   prank   ⎦

this must therefore be⟩
                    worker
⟨ up to   what the ~~child~~ dressed up
            what he had had to be in being born has made him so
in these skies — appeared — comes

to deliver in himself — in place of the

the priest the old man — who

will be haunted

---

* of a kind so inferior so not through himself, superior
for he crowds us, etc. ashes — now total —

until child that he had in him
(worker) * ~~who~~   in place of the priest — who
suffers needlessly from this confinement —
is hungry and thirsty (anger) cries out in the name
of justice, of being thus cloistered in the
priest ┼ priest (chaste and dying of hunger) chaste
child in him — dying of hunger, old.

          *returns pulling it along with him.....
mystery that one can know
only in solving it — love —
proof — child

{f 49 [34 (B)]}

Read.

12 people

Read. the

⎛ mass — the com/nion

⎝ each having

the volume I have decided on

⎛

⎝ — but assumed

paying 2 f. per pers. —
                effaced
at the price of the vol, heard

for nothing —

⌐ voice.   phonogr.

{f 50 [35 (B)]}

I am, as for me — faithful to the
book,
—

{f 51 [36 (A)]}

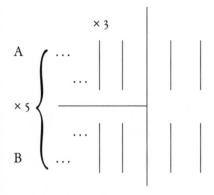

96 in place of 32 (72, of 24)

$\longrightarrow$

... in place of •
which restores these 3
to make three different
works? if the leaf has been
divided in 3

quintupling

two pl

Operat.

A   Read.
} the same wrk. is presented
B   twice differently
          reducing it to the same?

. . .

  . . .

= 6

= 12 half-l.

for 12 people   or 6 double seats   for

                                         both seatings

and . . .

. . .

same thing   only half   same day

= for 24 ppl.   set aside twice

                 the paper

(2 copies)

        me 25th.

     this 5 f. why?   5 francs?   25th seat

---

5 real francs — if I count them —

   to be able to see a work of which the price is —

                  the unity...

{f 53 [38 (A)]}

half
~~/~~ 10 doubles or 20 ~~de~~ singles
and then ~~20~~ per year. begin again

another book corresponding to that one —
on the 6

— which would make 3 years
3 times

— each year
120 leaves (1000 f. per leaf)

360 people
Year —

~~12 ppl~~

(1

importance — value (from which gilded edges)
be it
of paper   — a book, proportions at 5 or 6?
3
times in height its thickness spread out

and 4 times its width   the relation is in
base
thickness
the height indicates the number of lines   18

the width — their fragmented length   12

the thickness their sum —   either from 1 to 2/3

or if the height is reduced
to 12. total happens between the width and thickness
and the deduction from the number of lines   goldstamping above
indicates the number of volumes
which add up to one

---

from which 5 (or 6?) ~~books~~ volumes laid flat stacked

= the height of one upright — and a total of volumes

upright = ~~the height of~~ the block produced by one the

same number of vol. laid flat.   the block
~~identical~~
~~doubling the block laid flat or upright~~   #   = a book can thus
only contain
a quantity
of material — its
ideal value —
without number what-
ever it may be   maybe there is not
more or less   enough high or low — without val.
than that which is — the cost   from which infinite
it's too much and not enough.   — ideal — but value
(pure — diamond)

---

to study this after the verse   page | leaf   ~~book~~
volume
~~verse   piece~~
that ideally is
neither the book | verse   piece

126

(2

this block can only thus in any way make a square
façade, in seeing the backs, for example, whether upright
or laid flat — but it will not have it in depth or

it is kept in ~~it must be tripled, this block, upright~~
a rectangular
case — ~~or laid flat, tripling it in the sense of width~~
laws of this
rectangle ~~to form~~
about
proportions = in that which, when one considers it from the front will
become ~~the~~ <u>thickness</u>   (relation of ~~fatness~~

thickness
times two

of the book and of its width   laid flat or upright from which to

it is not fallen   signal it in gold — it remains the same
by accident   ~~its width, when in block, becomes its~~
sacred
to one alone —   ~~thickness~~
we emerge from it —   gold line, tracing it in
open it   thickness and width
on   given as exactly
thickness   as precisely as possible.

its width when, in block
becomes its thickness — and if we found
a disproportion in the block, upright, or
laid flat,
which is equivalent

separations   this would only be
of the book
which is opened   in this lack of width
disjunctions   (depth
of relations
of its different   born ~~no~~, in
measures   so much as thickness, not
width —

then, totally renouncing the
~~impersonal~~ square
whatever more could we do

127

(3

6 v or 12

or to divide it

would be to double, for example, this thickness —

edge to edge. and we would get from
in either sense, laid flat or upright
two blocks a <u>rectangle</u> presenting its

length equal to its width or 2 widths of vol.
or thickness
here —

each vol
becoming the
1st 6 × 6
36

a new side of
its surface ~~equal~~
such that 24:18 (width and thickness)
or 4:3
~~and as for~~

these six other vol. must be

the same — but presented differently —

(⌞ ⌟ ?)
or
⌟ ⌞

to establish an identity.

the Wk. in 6 v. being
given twice.

to fix a price

The readings having no other point
in

that of showing these scientific connections — discovery of the book
of its value ⁄

etc.

but in that same way identifying me as the author

constituting me in an act of audacious courage

(4

Concerning the one — who does not grasp the book

or its value.   ⌐   given itself, so fallen

from the sky and responding to all

                        — who can care for it

titled — etc.,

        as itself — ~~1~~st

           without revealing the author

      no — ⌐ the one who has written it

        No one — genius alone

   or if not the author the 1st reader

it is for who reads it — and last if he

grasps it —   it is an honor

                 to publish it

                    —

to find in that which precedes

the relations with 5 and 3 — Read.

{f 58 [43 (A)]}

and the book is pure block for this reader —

transparent — he reads inside, predicts it — knows

in advance — ~~your~~ ⌠ showing where it's — that which must be —

or finishing   ~~mute~~

joints — relations

{f 59 [44 (A)]}

folds ——

far here 20 vol.

feuilleton —

folds from each side

and for that reason
addition of one
leaf in sense inverse
against

returned, to the crease

death
rebirth?
for xxxxxxx

we never turn back
one fold in the other

sense — there is another leaf

to respond to the possibility

of this other sense

the fold which from one
side alone —
arrests the gaze —
and masks.

series of folds
gilded —
on stiff
cardboard (like
old bindings)

{f 60 [45 (A)]}

$= 96$
48-48

(288)

$\times 5 \mid 4 \times$ $\times 3$ $= 144 - 144$
$\times 5$

1440 p

$= 45$ leaves
$\times 2$
$90 \times 4 = 360$

$240 + 240 = 480$
$180 \quad 180 = 360$

5760p
240

25th

4 each
    year
        One of 4 books
        having 5 different
        motifs —
            distributed
            95 × 5
            =

{f 62 [47 (B)]}

It is essential that by
glancing over the succession
of phrases —
      With seating = leaf
— etc.
           everything appears
      according to this Program

That makes 1 vol of

320 (20 sheets of paper)

160 leaves

cut in 3

= 480

invitations —

with indication of nothing

---

                                        bouillon

384 over 20

   × 3

{f 65 [49 (B)]}

or 3 v. of 320
  if the leaves are
left uncut

{ff 67-73}
{f 68 [50 (B)]}

5 years. The Luster

{f 69 [51 (B)]}

placing itself at their will
in their seats
3 leaves
changeable

the question is of knowing
  titularies
  if the 24 come
 at the same time and only
 one reading
  ─────
  ─ or if
 or actually if 3
 readings are 8
  × 3
or 8 (with 2 assistants)

{f 70 [52 (B)]}

the manuscript alone
is mobile —
     it would be multiplied
     by 3

$$240,000$$
$$\underline{\quad\quad 3 \quad\quad}$$
$$720,000$$

24   25th
× 4   4
~~~~~~~~
96   = 100
× 500
~~~~~~~~
48000
        4   torn into 3
            from 3 vol
            into a run of 4000

{f 71v [53 (B)]}

is 3 too much ~~~~
immobilized
            and 1 lf.
    or
vol into 3 mobile lvs.?

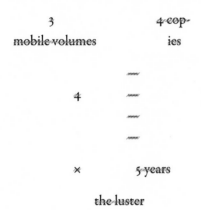

3   4 ~~cop-~~

~~mobile volumes~~   ies

4

×   ~~5 years~~

~~the luster~~

{f 72 [54 (B)]}

If volume triples
into 3 lvs — of which we
have demonstrated the use
binding them

1 lf for expenses
~~xxxxxx~~
materials —
2 lvs. remain for
me —

the two make a third
copy

{f 74 [55 (B)]}

the book suppresses
time   ashes

{f 75 [56 (B)]}

    toward the relation in
    of non coexistence

—————

      toward the relation
      of 8 printed pages

—————

the paper is only white if
    the sheet is virgin
          not
               the head

The hero
changes Dr. into
mystery — turns
dr. back into mystery
    — casts himself —
from which he gets the Idea —

and that which is in
            example
                vol.
the state of <u>Th</u> — he
turns it back into Hymn

{f 77 [58 (B)]}

Read.   (1
thus I myself make
        for the pleasure of
showing myself.   under a
                    pretext that —
                            the book
                                letter.

~~in the world~~

                    ⌐ for ⌐

(I could help myself
with the book precisely
by propagating it — I don't want,
        stop there
    — appear   so be it!

5

necessary to
dive back in and
repeat

2

I'm making   to show myself

                                    the one —

          in Idea   who knows
above all, s. ent.
        for we must assume

that of me — under this

appearance of study — that

                their action

                        tempts

                                alone —

                identifying myself

        in the book —

these remarks
           that in
the air
            spectacle
    eternal
dr̶ ̶a̶n̶d̶ ̶s̶y̶m̶p̶h̶o̶n̶y̶
̶a̶n̶ ̶a̶c̶t̶o̶r̶
            I
suddenly wonder
spring muslin
hopes of a single
sun   (against proofs
    it's that sickness   really
forced from being interested in it

{f 79 [60 (B)]}

3

a largeness in-
viting... people —
has tickets, etc . .   which
would like so much —
　　to acknowledge —

　in order to
find myself the only one
　　to come —

5

~~if not all that~~
~~truly they are~~
~~nothing sacred. The~~
~~proof war~~
        ~~murder~~
~~erected.~~
            ~~the only~~
~~happy crime~~

4

maybe
    — and to efface that —
for I am supposed to come
one of them —

   on what to base
the sum of invita-
tion
   — I am always
fixated —

6

~~so mediocre, to~~
~~kill another~~
~~erected~~
~~in glory~~

{f 81 [62 (B)]}

5

it's like a loan
above — if this works
in favor of the world
— to restore to the
people — in copies
at a good price

(with
my humble gain —

(1

~~The convent~~ we
~~become it all~~
did
~~same thing~~

with

~~it doesn't have~~
mass

6

and to replace booksellers
with beggars   oh
                concierge!)

— the Sum —
equaling this —

Consecration
divine presence
actor in front
remaining invisible
there

480
500
~~~~~~~~~~~~~~~
240 000

{f 84}

Read.
all is there

~~because it is not~~
~~finished~~
~~it's not possible~~
~~the cities were~~
~~the~~
all vain
crumbled
because

{f 86 [64 (B)]}

<table>
<tr><td></td><td></td><td>make</td></tr>
<tr><td>print no less</td><td colspan="2">The Text <s>edition of 400</s></td></tr>
<tr><td>10 times 4</td><td colspan="2">quadruple edition of 10</td></tr>
</table>

print no less

  10 times 4

    <s>If an edition of 400</s>

                                   make

                    The Text <s>edition of 400</s>

                    quadruple edition of 10

                        <s>assumed</s>   and 1 or 4 works

       <s>If kept for myself</s>   = 400 v.

              I attribute <s>some</s> to myself

              through my readings.

         the 10   copies or 40 v.

                              <s>leaving 360 vol.</s>

                              <s>or 90 copies</s>

— the 10 copies —

      to 10 Readings are each a variant.

(2

each seating
and me   being quadruple
9 people present × 4
at readings   = 36.

10 quadrupled seatings
in the amount of / 40 seatings times (360 seats
for 40 volumes
and 360 sheets
1 volume per seating
9 leaves for 9 seats.

each vol. has nine leaves
each seating has nine seats

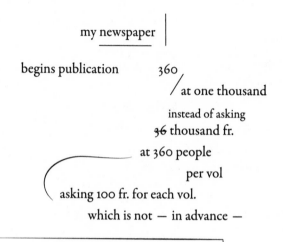

my newspaper

begins publication   360

at one thousand

instead of asking
~~36~~ thousand fr.

at 360 people

per vol

asking 100 fr. for each vol.

which is not — in advance —

I take 100 fr. Per copy 4 fr. making 5 times three

{f 89 [67 (B)]}

288	24
48	12

+ 12 me
recurring

{f 90 [68 (B)]}

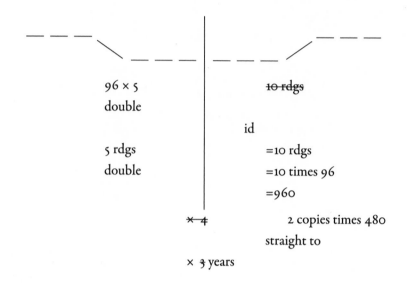

96 × 5
double

5 rdgs
double

id

~~10 rdgs~~

=10 rdgs
=10 times 96
=960

~~× 4~~

2 copies times 480
straight to

× ~~3~~ years

— — — | — — —

      — — — | — — —

1 1/2 leaves   that times 2

of 5   id   = 20 leaves

   1 leaf   leaves = 320

piece and leaf   × 3

       = 960

240 + 240

= 480

      = 6 Rgs

3 times

          = 24

     recommencing

      4 times (times 320)

24

people   war   crowd

seatings

me   nation theft

times 320   battle — marriage

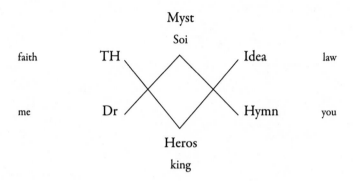

piece each
day —

360
___

20 fr /

7200 /

800
— 80
_____

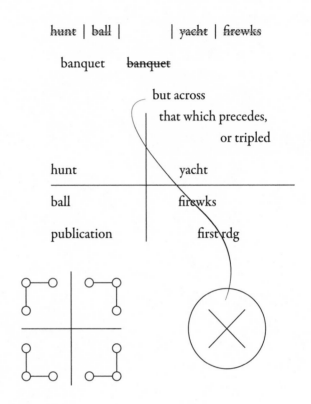

hunt | ball | | yacht | firewks

banquet   banquet

but across
that which precedes,
or tripled

hunt	yacht
ball	firewks
publication	first rdg

hunt
burial   baptism
banquet   yacht
ball   firewks.

hunt
  war   theft
      (marriage)
firewks

{f 95 [73 (B)]}

1, 10	4
− − −	36
9	

{f 96 [74 (B)]}

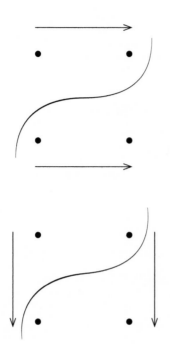

{f 97 [75 (B)]}

                                        Read.
              the print run diminishes
                   — ~~up to~~
                            and the paper
                   comes and takes the seat
                   —   up to a price
                   fusion of two
                                    minimum —
              stopping

              up to this moment there
              printing on fine paper
              or publishing separately
                            searching —

4

— and organs
~~re~~   literature
becomes exterior
so quickly, loses
quickly — the notion
— of mystery —
— that organs —

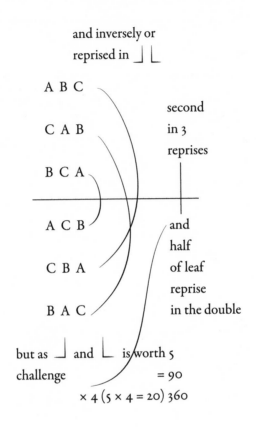

and inversely or
reprised in ⌋ ⌊

A B C

                second

C A B

                in 3

                reprises

B C A

A C B

                and
                half

C B A

                of leaf
                reprise

B A C

                in the double

but as ⌋ and ⌊ is worth 5
challenge   = 90
$$\times\ 4\ (5 \times 4 = 20)\ 360$$

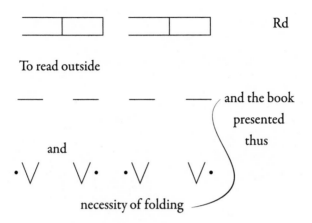

Rd

To read outside

and the book
presented
thus

and

necessity of folding

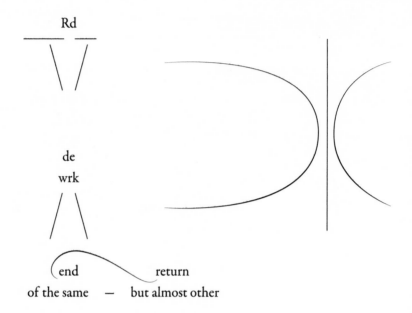

Rd

de
wrk

end   return
of the same   —   but almost other

each of the six concurrents
    3 for one wrk — 3
for the other is drawn from it
with its price of one ~~t~~housand
francs and it's the <u>same</u>
               from which 6000 f

which alone has had the idea
    of — of — these games —
    these —

yacht

— — —

Hunt	cloth
banquet	rifle

firewrk

theft — — —

— — —

mirage ball.
from which challenge, virgin)

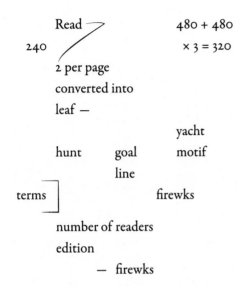

Read

240

2 per page
converted into
leaf —

480 + 480
× 3 = 320

yacht
hunt   goal   motif
            line
terms

            firewks

number of readers
edition
        — firewks

{f 104 [82 (B)]}

2 read. per year
    everyone inviting
        each other.

————

   week

————

240 p   from the page
         to the leaf
at 240 lvs.
        one side

S. of   Seatings
for Reading of the Dr
and of the Hymn.

        Th

    is

— by the hero

the development of the Dr
in ~~Th~~ the hymn ⌐ but
the hymn had to
be in the state of m

{f 106 [84 (B)]}

aced by the Dr.
     in case
someone attributes himself to it
     Th
     piece
     toward book

———————————

Seatings of Read
of the Dr and of the Hymn
— or of Myst. and Poetry

identical in the

Th. ⌈ or <u>Idea</u>

operated suppressed)

It suffices to satis-
fy
      our spirit —

with the equivalence
of light that con-
tains a ~~luster.~~

———

   The luster assures
     the Th.
which suffices the spirit.

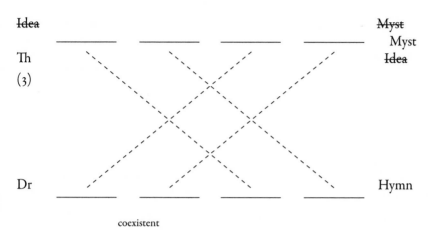

1/2 Dr 1 — 1/2 Myst 1 ;   while 1/2 Myst 2 ..

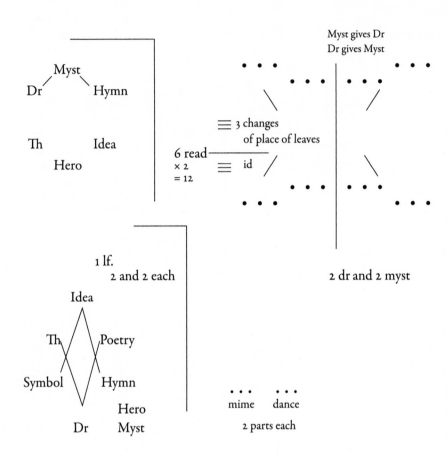

Each ~~The~~ text of the W is given two times

~~4 halves alone coexistent~~ ⟨are just same thing turned back
      and
   Myst ~~Is only~~ Dr ~~turned back~~   and presenting
     ,   Dr and myst.

the one outside what
the other hides inside

   Dr. the characters outside and Myst. inside
   ~~Myst~~

24 seats, foundation.

(in 8 times 3 = 24)

and the 25th is the operator

there are only 20 leaves:

consequently they

are not for the attendants

and the operator is counted among them.

(whatever the number of real
attendants, or even just the Reader
the operator

volumes   one,   each

These ~~four books~~ are ~~two~~

each

~~halves~~ two, ~~the~~ half of one

each

compared with ~~the~~ half of the other

~~in two different senses~~, which

thus provides two seatings.

20 v. of 384 — in 4 parts, either 5 by 5
(384 × 5 = 1920) or 1 piece. 2 = 3840 p. or
10 of 384. There are only 2 — which one time gives
2 pieces one meaning, another time 2 pieces another meaning.
The same text 2 times.

let's say   384 × 5 | 384 × 5

=

(the 384 being giveaways

complete or 96 × 4)

these   96   96   96   96   96
          A   B   C   d   e

= 480, or the greatest development
of a part, in so much as 1/4

[...]

{f 123 [100 (A)]}

2 leaves

| the title

on the verso
of the one — which becomes recto
— on the recto of
the other — which
becomes verso.
both
It shows thus
ing   — identity of the Book divined.

all that was taken from the leaf — in developing it —
light, that which escapes from it — all that is necessary
seeing on this virgin white in the blink of an eye.
without sign characters

we develop it — we stop ~~unti~~ just before
the grand ~~develop~~ interior overture, virg.
or we are going to know if something or nothing
other than all
that which is
double
even though developed   annul
she remains at the threshold
to write her repercussions
echo in the Pages

t-4 ~~and~~ this fact happe

[...]

{f 220 [169 (A)]}

He finds himself in a place-ancient City-where   from which he had prepared the
                                                         feast — (nuptials)
                                    Th   Dr
         The exploit which should bring him glory   is a crime: he stops
         —
time in this Operation; of which it is a miracle that the Invitation so well

understood by him, had sufficed the lady who made it for him without knowing it maybe. glow

(of that which inspired it in her)   genius — farce

                                     but to leave the Invitation without responding to it
                                                       order
                                     were it No —
and that the lady had feared   while she had at this point given herself to him
                                     one cannot —
what she did to him. Unknowingly

maybe. Agrees. hat   is a theft. virg. taken

         he covers her

                  in silk

                                     operation which is not

path
hospital
market
agony
gift —   Invitation to feast   Operation
sale
simple choice   If it is one
decoration   to everything except the meal   law it's that one
                                                  because one died
                 from which his hunger. The law goes quiet   without eating
                                        eats —   vow?
                     does not dare show herself thus   she veils herself   crime   (division
                                                       from the one.
                                                       is neither virg   which is neither - nor-
         Either   does not eat the lady

         to (let's suppose)   20 fr. for her   sale   vote

hunt   yacht   burial   marriage — baptism
                          place   decoration   bankruptcy
                       ancient City what is it?   prison   agony
ball.   fireworks   in
                       factory   school

195

                                        but... one has

factory   school   prison   never been able to know wh

                        satin — hat explodes

                                                                    sun

[...]

{f 245 [190 (A)]}

there are 8 pages
— 2 leaves —

Only the leaf counts,
makes the unity.
The leaf and the verse
The volume and the piece

the page:
the sign —
    this book

is itself abstract

———

1/2 lf.
the leaf
    1/4 of
= 2 ~~half~~ lvs.

that can triple itself
from one part and the other.

gesture tri

        page
page   ~~song~~
    hymn

and a double

leaf entire   3 1/2 lvs   3 1/2 lvs
                                    +
or 4 quarters   or 6 1/4 of l   or 6 1/4 of l.

and renewing it 4 times
96 × 4 = 384

```
    • • •            • • •
  • • • | • • •
  • • • | • • •
    • • •            • • •
```

~~and tripling once~~   ~~384 × 3 = 1152~~
                     the inverse
                then ~~the con-~~
                     ~~trary~~

and the whole 5 times   =   384 × 10
                             5 + 5

197

The seats — the furnishing.

curtain
enters, through the space left empty by the seats

The reader ~~arrives salutes to the right, in a~~
from right to left, and goes directly
~~glance, observes six seats, although doubles.~~
a little curved
~~retu~~ goes in ~~leaves~~ to the furnishing — of laquer —
~~which is divided thus~~ in half sight evidently
diagonal.

|||||

as follows

—

—

—

—

|||||

Each of these 6 drawers, on a diagonal,
containing 5 leaves (number easily visi-
ble in one look) — [those above upright
He knows, right away, and
one turn made to that which has
and those below laid flat? ~~He takes one~~
become his right,
turned from where he comes, ~~on by the left~~
is placed, under the single electric lamp, after having
first leaf ~~from the 1st draw~~ of five ~~from the first~~
taken one of each
drawer, above — ~~then turned toward the right~~
and below, holding these
six leaves

~~his right and an equal, below, that he holds in~~

by half

in each of his hands, the time ~~of the of en~~ of

those
~~confron~~ joining them, ~~her~~ inverted uprighted as

but   if the others

the first — as if he confronted the

suited
total format.

    He has in this moment ~~the~~ a number

of leaves equal to half the seats in the

auditorium. Let's say 6, and even though these

~~st~~ seats ~~can~~ are doubles, with one

special for an entitled, the leaves are

doubled into two leaves.   each leaf
of which the interior one.
becomes 8 pages — and 3 leaves = 24 pages)

He shows this, changing
~~He reunites 3 leaves~~ ~~He changes the 3 leaves~~

  ~~showing this:~~

~~leaf to leaf~~ the interior leaf of one to

the other leaf are the first ~~in two~~

two, the second two and third

placed momentarily to the side, <u>lit.</u>

⌈ unless returning three times

toward the left. (smile — wait) to whom appears

better this successive act — slightly veiled for the right

　　he successively takes the papers. ⌋

~~Is it always that he.~~　　　　　　　　up to the moment

when the whole rejoins, the operator, ~~goes~~ throws himself

right before him, from where he comes from, carrying
　　　　identifying himself
(toward the voice which reads) this fascicle as
　　　　for each.
to him. ~~(while identifying himself,~~

　　The whole has lasted three quarters of an hour — one

quarter of an hour interval (new
　　　　　　　as attempted from the beginning
timbre, glow)

　　　　　　　and

　　　　　　⌈ total 2 h

returned this time from the operator ~~for the~~
bringing the volume thus composed —
~~in order to redistribute it evidently, i to d~~

                            ~~to the drawers, in~~
i.[t's] to d.[istribute]   ~~block~~
an inverse operation

performed ~~a part of the~~ relatively in the
second part of the auditorium. He will
read it ~~and the~~ thus and will redistribute it to the
drawers but inverse   ~~like a~~

                                   ||||

                             —

                    —

            —

      —

||||

                                        where it seems

——— Such is the double seating.
having shown the identity of this volume with
self   and the
~~itself~~: it is comprised of 24 people,
each having a given moment

It represented one of the leaves. — or the
12 seats the twelve leaves (pages that can only be
separated from the leaves in order to
interpolate them through an exchange and that's it)

⌐ electr light purity —
          — the volume, despite the fixed im-
pression, becomes by this game, mobi-
le — from death it becomes life

So that all that which is there in block.
happens there. there must be 5 readings, making 96 ×
5 = 480 × 2 = 960 pages (with 480)
                    double price.
              establishment of the price
                    and the 100 lvs

—

A second series of reading can be given in the
inverse sense ↗ then ↘

ACKNOWLEDGMENTS

Grateful acknowledgment is made to the editors of

Lana Turner: A Journal of Poetry and Opinion, the Poetry Society

of America website, and *Volt,* where versions of these translations

first appeared.

Special thanks to Suzanna Tamminen for her support of this work.

ABOUT THE AUTHOR

STÉPHANE MALLARMÉ was a major French poet and critic of the nineteenth century, a leader of the Symbolist movement whose work anticipated many revolutionary artistic schools of the twentieth century, such as Cubism, Dadaism, Futurism, and Surrealism. He was recognized during his lifetime as one of the greatest French poets, though his obscure and often impenetrable style of expression made him difficult to understand. Mallarmé's weekly salons, through which he exerted considerable influence on the next generation of artists, were considered the heart of Parisian intellectual life and drew writers such as Yeats, Rilke, and Valéry.

ABOUT THE TRANSLATORS

BLAKE BRONSON-BARTLETT earned his PhD in English in the English Department at the University of Iowa in 2014. He is currently a postdoctoral teaching fellow at Technische Universität Dortmund. He is the editor of a volume of essays on the nonfiction writings works of Walt Whitman for the online Nineteenth-Century Literature Criticism series (2013).

ROBERT FERNANDEZ is the author of the volumes of poetry *We Are Pharaoh* (2011), *Pink Reef* (2013), and *Scarecrow* (2016). He is the recipient of a New American Poet Award and has been an editor for the PEN Poetry Series. His poems have appeared in the *New Republic, Lana Turner, Poetry, Hambone, A Public Space,* and elsewhere.